Political Psychology

"New Ideas for Activists"

Donald L. Conover

Words Matter, LLC
Suite 130, 3 Church Circle
Annapolis, MD 21401
410-919-7571

Designed by ME Design

Manufactured in the United States of America

Printed by CreateSpace, An Amazon.com Company
Available from Amazon.com and other online stores
Available on Kindle and other devices.

Library of Congress Cataloging-in-Publication Data
Conover, Donald L.
Conover, Skip
Political Psychology
/Donald L. Conover

ISBN: 978-0-9907726-2-0

PREFACE

This book is about using psychological concepts for political activism. It is intended for politicos of all stripes, left or right; green, black or white; Christian, Jew, or Muslim; male or female; fundamentalist or pacifist. It is primarily informed by the work of Dr. Carl G. Jung, who many regard as the greatest psychologist of the 20th Century.

There are many books with the title Political Psychology. Most of them are written by licensed Jungian analysts or licensed psychotherapists. While those books may contain some things for political activists, it is very difficult to separate the wheat from the chaff for this purpose, because they often get bogged down in psychotherapeutic mumbo jumbo, and they rarely give true guidance to the person who wants to see true and sustainable change in the world on the entire spectrum of political
issues.

The sole purpose of this book is to show by example how to "change the frame" so that political issues can be understood in a new way, in a new context, and beyond the same old tired rhetoric that we see on our cable television channels.

This book is most emphatically not about psychotherapy, and it is not intended to be useful to anyone suspecting they may be suffering from the onset of some mental illness. If you feel that you may be so afflicted, the best I can do is urge you to see a mental health professional, who will be best equipped to set you on the right path to recovery. I am not a licensed therapist. I make no pretensions along those lines. Furthermore, I never intend to become a mental health professional.

All of those caveats notwithstanding, I have been studying the works of Dr. Carl G. Jung in detail since 1987, when I was first introduced to the Myers-Briggs Type Indicator ("MBTI"). The MBTI is a personality test based on

Dr. Jung's Psychological Types, published in 1921, but including essays dating back to 1913. This test and the teachings surrounding it are exceedingly useful in understanding the needs and attitudes of the people around you. During my 23-year career in the U.S. Marine Corps and U.S. Marine Corps Reserve, from which I retired with the rank of Lieutenant Colonel, I found that the Armed Forces of the United States uses the MBTI in every senior school I encountered, including the Marine Corps Command and Staff College, the Naval War College, the Industrial College of the Armed Forces, and the National War College. In the armed forces it is a useful methodology for teaching how to organize a team to complete a specific mission based on the personalities of military personnel, but those issues Dr. Jung's work is out of favor among therapists, because it provides no quick fixes. It is not oriented toward giving someone a pill to solve a problem like depression. That is the quick way to get someone out of the healthcare system, but in my opinion it does nothing for solving the underlying issues people face in their everyday life, and in dealing with the forces alive in their psyche. A true solution to an underlying neuroses can take many psychotherapy sessions to identify and address in a truly.

Since 1987, thanks especially to the work of Dr. Clarissa Pinkola Estes, Dr. Jean Shinoda Bolen, Dr. Jean Raffa, Dr. Sonu Shamdasani, Dr. Ellen S. Kaye Gehrke, Dr. Jennifer Lilla, Dr. Martha Crawford, Mr. Lewis Lafontaine, Mr. C.V. Posing, Author Meltem Arikan, Actress Pinar Ogun, Actor Memet Ali Alabora, Actress Salma Hayek, Actor Ed Harris, and Artists John Ebersberger, Frieda Kahlo, Diego Rivera, Jackson Pollock, Vincent Van Gogh, Pierre-Auguste Renoir, and many others, including the many members of the Carl Jung Depth Psychology page on Facebook, I have come to understand the deep significance of Dr. Jung's work across the whole spectrum of human endeavor.

Dr. Jung's work can be daunting! He wrote an entire shelf of books, and this prodigious scholarship is beyond comprehension to mere mortals like the rest of us. He had his own "Confrontation with the Unconscious" beginning in 1913, and wrestled with it in a private collection of writings and personal artwork until 1930. This collection did not become public until 48 years after his death, in 2009, when Dr. Sonu Shamdasani won the permission of Dr. Jung's heirs to publish it as The Red Book.

It was only from reading The Red Book that I understood that I had experienced my own confrontation with the unconscious in 1993. This manifested in a novel I wrote and published online under a pseudonym. The heroine in my novel woke me at 6:00 a.m. every day for eight months, and would not allow me to rest until I typed at least 500 words of the novel. It was exactly like taking dictation. There was no element of it that came from my conscious mind.

Thanks to my exposure to Dr. Jung's work, I now know that the heroine was a manifestation of my anima, and the contents of the work were manifestations of a part of my "shadow" as defined by Dr. Jung. Well over 100,000 people have read all or part of my novel online in 18 languages. Most of them do not know it was my work, although many of my close friends do know. It is not formally published anywhere, though it is beloved by many.

In 1995 I had an urge to paint. I had never been competent at drawing, so it took great courage to buy my first set of paints. For the next ten years I painted nearly every day, and in the process "invented" two new styles of painting, which later turned out to be neither new nor unique, but rather manifestations of the archetypes and collective unconscious, which Dr. Jung wrote about through his long career. I found that whenever I was painting regularly my life ran rather smoothly, but when I stopped, things mysteriously did not work out as well.

Since 2005 I have devoted my creativity to my writing and business career, and to curating the Archetype in Action™ Organization website. Although I have experienced many of the bumps and trials of the financial collapse of 2008, I attribute whatever successes I have had to the fact that I have continued to access the creativity of my unconscious Soul through my writing. This has given me the drive to write several books, some of which are still unpublished.

There is no substitute for reading the work of Dr. Carl Jung directly. There are hundreds if not thousands of books written about him, but if you do not read his work directly, it will be like seeing the shadow instead of the substance of something. If you are a layman, I urge you to start with Man and His Symbols, which Dr. Jung had completed for laymen late in his life, and Memories, Dreams, Reflections, which is as close as Dr. Jung ever came to writing a memoir. These are in normal language, are readily available in your local bookstore, and do not require a deep knowledge of the many concepts he introduced to understand them, and you will find them useful in your life immediately.

Your next reading should be in Symbols of Transformation (1911-12/1952), which was originally published in English in 1916 under the name Psychology of the Unconscious. I found it very useful to read this earlier version via audio recording from Audible.com on my iPhone. Another valuable overview source is Dr. Jung's Introduction to Secret of the Golden Flower, which is based on original translations of the philosophy of the I Ching by Richard Wilhelm. These help put the entire development of human psychology into context, and fundamentally show that all human beings are made from the same basic psychic content.

As you reach the intermediate stage of your study of Dr. Jung's teachings, you can then hope to understand The Red Book, in which editor Dr. Sonu Shamdasani provided a very useful and comprehensive Introduction, to help the reader appreciate the content. It is very important that you see the full volume, which contains all of the images Dr. Jung painted, although there is a less expensive "Reader's Edition" also available, but contains none of the images. Under no circumstances should this book be taken up as a starting point. As Dr. Jung rightly said himself in 1959:

"To the superficial observer, it will appear like madness. It would also have developed into one, had I not been able to absorb the overpowering force of the original experiences. ... I always knew that these experiences contained something precious, and therefore I knew nothing better than to write them down in a 'precious,' that is to say costly, book and to paint the images that emerged through reliving it all-as well as I could." From the Epilogue to The Red Book, by Dr. Carl Jung.

Skip Conover, August 2014

FOREWORD

There's a Cherokee legend that goes like this:

An old Cherokee is teaching his grandson about life. "A fight is going on inside me," he said to the boy.

> "It is a terrible fight and it is between two wolves. One is evil - he is anger, envy, sorrow, regret, greed, arrogance, self-pity, guilt, resentment, inferiority, lies, false pride, superiority, and ego." He continued, "The other is good - he is joy, peace, love, hope, serenity, humility, kindness, benevolence, empathy, generosity, truth, compassion, and faith. The same fight is going on inside you - and inside every other person, too." The grandson thought about it for a minute and then asked his grandfather, "Which wolf will win?" The old Cherokee simply replied, "The one you feed."

From a Cherokee Legend (www.firstpeople.us)

Donald "Skip" Conover is like that old Cherokee grandfather. He is a husband, father and grandfather who observes the battle between his inner wolves and cares about the legacy he'll leave for his grandchildren and beloved country. He is also a Viet Nam vet with 23 years of service in the United States Marine Corps, attorney, successful business entrepreneur, world traveler, artist, author, creator of the Archetype in Action™ Organization, and blogger. A man of vast life experience, he's met a lot of wolves, good and evil alike.

With this book, a compilation of blog posts from over three years, he directs our attention to some of them. His primary focus is on the most powerful and corrupt wolves in America's political and economic institutions, people who will do and say anything to manipulate the way we think to their own advantage.

Some are arrogant, power-hungry "Masters of the Universe" who pound their messages into our brains via the media in order to control major voting blocks of the global electorate. How many of us have noticed that the relentless televised harangues about issues like abortion, gay rights and evolution divert our attention away from what is important to our national and global welfare? As an example, Conover cites the massive amounts of time and money that CNN, Fox News and other reporting organizations devoted to the mysterious disappearance of Malaysian flight MH370 while almost completely ignoring the serious threat posed to the world by the Russian takeover of Crimea occurring at the same time. Other evil wolves are the greedy and tyrannical "1%ers," like the Wall Street investment bankers whose manipulations severely compromised the world's economy for the sole purpose of fortunes. As one of the millions of Americans who was robbed of his life savings and enslaved by debt because of their selfish machinations, Conover directs some of his most scathing remarks to them.

Then there are the superior and self-important wolves, who would perpetuate the inequality of women with laws that would deny them basic rights. Or the repressive wolves, who orchestrated the violent actions by police forces across the United States against the Occupy Wall Street demonstrators, thus undermining everyone's Constitutional Rights of Freedom of Assembly and Freedom to Petition Government for a Redress of Grievances. A patriot who loves America and vigorously defends the diversity which made it great, Conover writes to show us our blind spots and help us curb our prejudices before the evil within and without destroys our freedoms. In these brief and timely essays he illustrates his messages with a history lesson here, a YouTube video there, or an example from his personal life. In recent years Conover has been an avid student of the famous Swiss psychologist, Dr. Carl G. Jung. As such, he places the ultimate blame for the chaos created by the evil wolves in today's world squarely where it belongs: on our psychological ignorance and complacency. Like the wise Cherokee grandfather, he wants us to know our inner realities. To that end he peppers his astute observations about the news of the day with pertinent quotes from the father of Depth Psychology:

"Only an infantile person can pretend that evil is not at work everywhere, and the more unconscious he is, the more the devil drives him. It is just because of this inner connection with the black side of things that it is so incredibly easy for the mass man to commit the most appalling crimes without thinking. Only ruthless self-knowledge on the widest scale, which sees good and evil in correct perspective and can weigh up the motives of human action, offers some guarantee that the end-result will not turn out too badly." Dr. Carl G. Jung, Aion, ¶ 255

"Who is the real enemy? Whisper who dares!" Conover's mantra throughout this well-informed and thought-provoking book challenges us to see "good and evil in correct perspective." This task is especially relevant now that the painfully divisive 2012 presidential election is behind us and the 2016 election season is about to begin.

There is hope for America and the world, but our future hinges on what may be the most important question of our time: "Which wolf will I feed?"

Jean Benedict Raffa
Author of the Wilbur Award-winning Healing the Sacred Divide

INTRODUCTION

Today's news media, both in the United States and around the world, like nothing better than a good argument. The interest and emotions arguments provoke drive people to watch their programs, and help them sell advertising; nothing more. But do they change anything?

Their constant harangues and poll results, reported like box scores in a baseball game, are touted as though they were the most important thing ever, and oh how we must watch this debate or that pundit, or we will miss something. Not!

The loyal viewers of MSNBC or FoxNews are largely the converted to the Left or to the Right, who are only looking for validation of their own opinions, which rarely change.

Arguments do nothing but entrench people in their opinions. They do not change the opinions of the opposing side. Polls give the general view of a small sample of people, but they do not tell us what will happen in the only poll that matters, at the polling place on election day. Mitt Romney's pollsters had him convinced that he would win by a good margin in the 2012 Presidential Election in the United States. Who can say why? The successes and failings of pollsters is not my topic here.

The point is that political changes cannot come from constant harangues and debate. They can only come when people see the need for change themselves, and call for those changes or at least acquiesce to them. Many have called this reframing the issue, and that description is as appropriate as any.

The gun debate is a good case in point. My gun toting friends keep expressing a fear that the government will come and take their guns. With over 300 million guns in the United States, this would not be possible, but this is nonetheless their fear and they will not be dissuaded from it.

But change in how we deal with guns will come, no matter what the talking heads say and what politicians do on either side. One example of changing the frame would be to persuade personal liability insurance companies that they should make their policies invalid if a gun is not kept in a secure location in private homes.

The Newtown tragedy might have been averted if only Nancy Lanza had kept her firearms under lock and key. Insurance companies like such provisions, because they mean that they have an excuse for not paying or not defending an insured. Nancy Lanza might even still be alive today, if she had followed that simple precaution. Of course, if she had lived, she might well have been sued by all of the families of those lost at Newtown, and unless that provision was in her liability insurance policy, the insurance company might well have had to pay to the full extent of the policy.

Such a change would require no public debate and no legislation. When was the last time you listened to a debate about a change in a single term of an insurance policy? The owners of insurance companies should love such changes, because such provisions would make it difficult for them to be drawn into embarrassing cases like Newtown, where their insured was negligent.

Another example of reframing the issue came up when my wife and I lived in Washington, DC. We lived on a street where there were known drug dealers. Their "drug house" was raided by police several times while we lived there, but the police never found anything. Why? Because there were informants inside the police department, who would warn them of any raid.

These were pretty silly dealers, though, because even though they were running a multi-million dollar enterprise, they didn't pay their water bill. When the water company shut off the water to their house, the bathtubs and other receptacles got filled up with things we don't want to think about, and then the place began to stink. The next door neighbor called the health department, which blocked all of the doors and windows with cinder block and condemned the property. Amazing! No guns, no police cars, no debate, no informants, no trial, no more drug house, and the traffic on our street dropped in half. Problem solved! Political issues are just like that.

Many of my essays are on reframing the issue. They are not meant to provide a specific rule, which is always correct, but only to provide examples of how political issues can be reframed to make us look at them another way. I warn you though, if you look at any issue from another perspective, you might start to find yourself changing your side in a decades old argument. Are you willing to risk that in order to see changes gravitate toward your way of thinking? If not, then read no more! Simply go back and submerse yourself in the cacophony of the talking heads on the "news" channels. They abound! If so, then read on! I've written a lot to give you the idea of what you can do.

Political Psychology

Chapter 1. Our Task in America:
The Lesson of Apollo 13

**America represents the essence of the human spirit allowed to develop
to its fullest potential.**

Many Americans are totally disgusted by the way things have gone in our
politics recently. The Red State/Blue State duality has created a national neurosis of the first order, and instead of helping us heal our divide, commentators like Bill O'Reilly on the right and Chris Matthews on the left just seem
to want to drive us into a frenzy of hate for our fellow countrymen. Indeed,
Matthews often says about the political fight, "I love this stuff," with a self
satisfied grin.

Duality is normal in the human psyche. Without a range of opposites to
energize our lives, nothing happens. But sometimes things get pushed too
far in one direction or another and healing is required. That was the case at
the time of The Civil War and it is the case in America today.

The origin of our unique national neurotic disease is simple to diagnose. It
was quite natural for Americans to react in a defensive way after the 9/11
attacks. While we can find reasons to hate one another politically, Americans
know that there is some essence of our country that is worth fighting for
together despite our differences. Though it may be difficult to define that
essence, it emerged instantaneously in symbolic form. American flags flew
off the shelves, and many cars drove down the road with flags flying in the
hurricane force wind of our national highways.

But the wounds to our national sense of self from the 9/11 attacks were mild
compared to the wounds of being taken into the Iraq War by political lies,

and the crash of our economy caused by the unconscionable frauds of Wall Street investment bankers. These last two events amounted to an explosion in our American psyche, which the divisive talking heads and their venal masters have been exploiting ever since, as if they were promoting a Super Bowl game.

So how do we heal our national divide, and restore America to its greatness in the world? The movie "Apollo 13" illustrates some useful answers. When an explosion occurred aboard the spacecraft headed for the Moon, the NASA leaders were faced with the crisis of creating a new attitude. Instead of putting two more men on the Moon, they had to come up with a new mission--how to get the Apollo 13 crew back to Earth safely. Our national task, if we will save the best of America, is just like that. We cannot continue with the America we all love without envisioning something new.

"What do we have on the ship that is good?" That was the question Mission Director Gene Kranz (Ed Harris) asked of his fellow flight controllers after the explosion aboard Apollo 13. Like Kranz, we must ask ourselves, "What do we have in America that is good? **"What is the essence of America** for which we would all fight, regardless of whether we paint our faces red or blue; regardless of our race, our gender, our religion, our national origin or the size of our bank account?

The immortal scene of finding a way to put a square filter into a round hole aboard Apollo 13 sums up the difficulty we face in finding that American essence.

This video can be found on Youtube as "Apollo 13 (7/11) Movie Clip – Square Peg in a Round Hole (1995)"

But Americans have never shrunk from adversity. All of us are here because we, or our ancestors saw something good in America. Even if we were born here after many generations, our lives have been blessed and infused with that fundamental essence. Like the engineers who saved the Apollo 13 astronauts, we have the can-do spirit that can heal our national neurosis.

It's quite clear that we need to envision our leaders as healers rather than dividers. Once we do that, we will **find that something new which defines the essence of America once again.** No, we will not be as innocent in our views as we were before 9/11, but we will be able to enjoy our new level of maturity, **which will allow the America we love to continue to emerge as the essence of the human spirit allowed to develop to its fullest potential.**

Chapter 2:
Outgrowing Our Political Divide

Many of us despair at how the United States has descended into its current horrendous political divide. Fortunately, I am confident that we shall overcome the rift. This confidence comes from a few truths I know about the American spirit.

We have had great divides before. The American Civil War was the bloodiest, but in my lifetime divides have emerged as the Civil Rights Movement, Women's Rights Movement, and the Vietnam War Protests most notably. The good news is that we outgrow them and move on   .

Psychologists know that very often neuroses are not "cured" but rather outgrown. We learn more about what it takes to succeed in the world, we bring some of our own internal debates into consciousness, and we adapt.

I recall how angry I was when President Jimmy Carter granted unconditional amnesty to those who avoided service during Vietnam. At the time I regarded such men as cowards, and I did not feel that they deserved to take advantage of the many benefits of citizenship, when others of their fellow Americans had died in the line of duty.

In retrospect, though, I know that President Carter made the right call. Failure to resolve the issue and embrace our fellow citizens would have meant years of divisive trials and separations of families, which would not have been beneficial to the United States. I admit that I feel resentment when some of those artful dodgers are considered in Presidential politics, but I have outgrown my resentment enough to be able to reconcile myself to their leadership.

The strength of our Country has always come from its Diversity. We count as Americans people from every national origin, race, religion, and cultural group. This has been the great crucible, which has forged the steel of the American spirit when we face the rest of the world. Every time a good idea emerges from any group, we all adopt it very quickly. When a bad idea emerges, though, we all work to remove it from the system, fighting our causes both pro and con, until the Truth finally emerges. Other countries don't allow bad ideas to be challenged as readily which means they do not develop their societies as quickly. The results speak for themselves.

Part of our consternation this year is that several issues we thought were already pressed out of the system have reared their ugly heads. The most significant of these is our Freedom of Religion. Suddenly we have a large minority of our Country, who want to use their brand of Christianity to dominate the rest of us. Many of today's Americans are descended from people who came to North America to get away from religious warfare. Those of us who remember this fact will not allow any brand of Christianity or any other religion to dominate the rest of us, no matter how many people have been converted. That is a pathway back to the Middle Ages, which we will not countenance.

A woman's right to abortion has always been a divisive issue, because it is so emotional. There is no human being, who can think of the idea of abortion and not be saddened by its necessity. Nonetheless, for many sensible reasons, women have aborted their pregnancies for various reasons for thousands of years. Unfortunately, before Roe v. Wade, many of those procedures resulted in the death of the woman.

My Mother told me on her deathbed (she wanted to be sure I knew) that my two Grand Mothers had 5 abortions between them in the 1920s. She wanted me to know because of the horrible impact on our society from those necessities. Conservative women like my Grand Mothers were obliged to sneak about and commit felonies, and some estimates said that 16% of the medical community also committed felonies on a regular basis.

Today, the venal politicians that keep the abortion issue alive do so because of its emotional power, counting on the fact that women under 50 will not remember how bad things were before the U.S. Supreme Court made its decision. They know that making abortion illegal again will not save a single baby, because women will find ways to have the abortions they need, but they can use the issue for its emotional value to drive a wedge in our society for other reasons having nothing to do with women's reproductive rights.

Dr. Carl Jung talked about the concept of enantiodromia, which is defined as the tendency of things to turn into their opposite. As I have watched politics over my lifetime, it does give me some reason for optimism. We have seen this in my lifetime, where the Democratic Party became the Republican Party in the South.

In the 1950s and 1960s and before the South was dominated by the Democratic Party. Attitudes in that part of our Country have changed some in the years since, but now the Republican Party has taken on the mantle of hate and bigotry. This year the rhetoric seems particularly bad, but I am pleased to note that some members of the Republican Party do show some signs that common sense will prevail once again, once our divisive Election 2012 is behind us, and I am confident that the powers of the Republican Party will steer it back toward a centrist point of view.

How long will it take America to outgrow misogyny, hatred and bigotry? I cannot say, but I know in my heart that America will lead the world into a new perspective about humanity at large, and about global thinking. We will all set aside the hatreds that have divided humanity for so long, and accept that we all live on the same very precious and fragile blue sphere in the infinity of our Universe.

Chapter 3: Is the American Psyche a Neurotic Mess?

"The neurotic fled from his duties, and his libido withdrew from the tasks imposed by real life. In consequence, the libido became introverted and directed towards an inner life. The libido followed the path of regression. To a large extent fantasies replaced reality, because the patient refused to overcome certain real difficulties. Unconsciously the patient prefers, and very often consciously too, his dreams and fantasies to reality. To bring him back to real life and the fulfillment of its necessary duties the analysis proceeds upon the same false path of regression that has been taken by his libido. So that at the beginning of psychoanalysis it looks like it is supporting the morbid tendencies of the patient." Dr. Carl G. Jung

Neurosis is often caused by a trauma, which leads to a regression back to an earlier stage of personality development. Those who overcome the neurosis go on to lead a normal mature life, but those who don't create fantasies, which have their own fantasy life. Those fantasies are not well adapted to the real world, so they create a world of their own, which is often unsuitable for the world at large.

We Americans have every right to be neurotic as a description of our national character. After the trauma of the 9/11 attacks, it was normal for us to run home to Daddy in the form of our national military. But have we forgotten what it means to be an American? Have we given up the very essence of America in our neurotic quest to protect it?

On September 25, 2001, Professor Peter Ferrara of George Mason University School of Law published "What Is An American?" in the National Review Online. This piece was later republished and spread around the world as "To Kill an American". At the time, Americans loved this, because **"Americans are not a particular people from a particular place. They are the embodiment of the human spirit of freedom. Everyone who holds to that spirit, everywhere, is an American."**

But sadly, since 9/11, the trauma has been used by the forces of regression to back Americans down from our great vision of the future for our Country and people the world over. Those forces have sold us fantasies that are untrue.

It is no longer true that we have the best healthcare, the best education, and the best freedoms in the world. The statistics are quite clear on these points. But many of my countrymen want to give up our freedoms of religion, press, speech, assembly, and petition to dishonorable men, who would and have already snatched these freedoms from us. We only need to remember the brutal behavior of police forces across the country last fall to realize the truth of that. I can go on chapter and verse about how the wealthy have diluted our democracy, but I won't. Election 2012 is about nothing if not about that!

Oh yes, we still have the largest economy and military establishment in the world, but, as a nation, we have coasted on the dominance of The Greatest Generation. There is a new day dawning, when people around the world want what we have, and many of them have the means to get it, either peaceably or otherwise. We will either have to lead, or get out of the way.

As a remedy to our neurosis, I can offer nothing better than the thought of the old Cherokee Chief in his story of "Two Wolves":

One evening an old Cherokee Chief told his grandson about a battle that goes on inside people. He said, 'My son, the battle is between two 'wolves' inside us all   .
One is Evil. It is anger, envy, jealousy, sorrow, regret, greed, arrogance, self-pity, guilt, resentment, inferiority, lies, false pride, superiority, and ego.

The other is Good. It is joy, peace, love, hope, serenity, humility, kindness, benevolence, empathy, generosity, truth, compassion and faith.'

The grandson thought about it for a minute and then asked his grandfather: 'Which wolf wins?' The old Cherokee Chief simply replied, 'The one you feed."

My fellow Americans: Which wolf will you feed in 2014? Just askin'!

Chapter 4: Osama bin Laden Destroyed America and It's Not Coming Back

Humpty Dumpty sat on a wall,
Humpty Dumpty had a great fall;
All the king's horses and all the king's men
Couldn't put Humpty together again.

The Dorling Kindersley Book of

Nursery Rhymes (2000)

Much of the angst many Americans feel with the 2012 Election has to do with the fact that we all feel that we lost something precious about our country in the 9/11 attacks, and we have not been able to get it back. In the deluded mind of Osama bin Laden was the idea that, if he committed a monstrous act of terrorism, fellow Muslims would rise up against America and destroy it. He was wrong. We destroyed it ourselves.

Dr. Carl Jung described the archetype behind bin Laden's kind of behavior as "The Trickster". In his warped mind, Osama bin Laden imagined that he could reverse the hierarchical order of civilization by committing what, for him, amounted to a malicious prank.

There are always unexpected consequences. In place of the return of the Caliphate he imagined, Osama bin Laden brought down on the Muslim World the wrath of the United States of America. That in turn created a problem for humanity as a whole in the form of a chain of psychological events, which still have not been brought into proper perspective.

The first of these psychological events was to constellate The Warrior archetype in all able-bodied Americans. Those who were too old or "busy" to take up arms cheered from their couches as thousands of Americans took up arms against our enemies, whoever they were. The problems engendered included the murder of tens of thousands innocents, who were not our enemies; the increase of the American defense budget beyond our ability to pay; and ultimately the near collapse of the global economy as a whole. We thereby created a like number of new enemies and a dependence on those defense budgets because they mean jobs we otherwise are unable to create, because, in the chaos, greedy Wall Street was allowed to over reach, creating investment vehicles with more risk than a roll of the ball in Roulette.

The result is that we now have millions of fellow Americans, who have lost their life's savings, and who are naturally looking for a magician to put things back the way they were. The Truth is, though, that Americans can never go back to the way we were. Too many things have changed for the worse.

Our industries have been given to China and other developing countries.

Our religions are broken to the extent that they promote intolerance and insist on "faith" in positions that deny science. Their insistence on militant ignorance simply impoverishes our hope of having a competitive country in the future, since other countries don't hesitate to train their citizens in scientific reality.

Yes, we do need a military, but why does its cost need to be twice as big as before 9/11? We have increased the size of the defense budget by more than $300 billion per year. That's more than $3 trillion since 9/11. What have we gotten for that? Where has the money been going? During the decade, we have put only one aircraft carrier into service at an approximate cost, including air wing, of $10 billion. Increasing the size of the Marine Corps by 27,500 men increased the cost by about $27.5 billion, even if you say fielding each Marine costs $1 million over the 10-year period. Visible large increases in the Air Force and Army are likewise absent, so where is all of this money going?

From the end of the Cold War until 9/11, Americans lived in a kind of bubble, where they did not have to or did not want to worry about the rest of the world. It wasn't the first time. After World War I, the U.S. Army was reduced to 137,000 officers and men, and during the 1930s Americans were more worried about economic conditions than what was happening in Germany and Japan, where venal leaders were using the economic frustrations of their populations to build military strength. The result was a similar burst of the bubble in the form of the Pearl Harbor attacks.

The Truth is that America can never return to those bubbles. The world has become too small a place, thanks to global travel, the Internet, Facebook, Twitter and globalization generally. If America is to lead the rest of the world in the future, Americans are going to have to dare to make it lead once again. This means persuading religious groups to update their messages into the 21st Century and stop promoting militant ignorance; it means keeping our military vigilance, but not frittering away hundreds of billions of dollars on bogeymen; and it means finding reasonable ways for banks to operate like banks once again, rather than like croupiers at a global crap game.

What is the best answer for the future?

When American Astronaut Frank Borman took "Earthrise" on December 24, 1968, it became the symbol for humanity's future for the next millennium. Humanity must learn to live together, because we have no place else to go. Mankind has been slow to see the significance of this symbol: "Earthrise"- by Astronaut Frank Borman, NASA, December 24, 1968 aboard Apollo 8.

The American space program, of which Borman was a part, had created over a million private sector jobs and completed a prodigious amount of science and engineering in the preceding decade. Why can't we do great things like that again? I notice, as a point of fact, that as a percentage of GDP, we now spend only 1/3 as much on NASA as we did during the run-up to landing on the moon. We currently spend only about 1/50th as much on NASA as we do on the Defense Department. That seems far too little, considering the private sector jobs that are possible thanks to a major space mission and highlights only one of thousands of sectors where America can and should lead again.

We simply must stop believing the myth that we can somehow return to some ideal mythological space where men were men and women were women, and all of the children were above average. We've been investing in our fears not our hopes for too long.

How can we teach Americans to lead the world once again? One thing I know is that it won't be by putting Humpty Dumpty back together again. We are going to have to build a new world, with new ideas of how we will live and work together in peace. All of us, in our heart of hearts, know that the status quo is untenable. We need to stop investing in our fears and start dreaming again.

Your ideas are welcome.

Chapter 5: "If They Give You Lined Paper, Write the Other Way"

"Words are like wild animals."
Dr. C.G. Jung

While I have some mixed emotions about the "Anonymous Movement," one of their points I agree with entirely. That is the thought that, "You can't kill an idea!" Once an idea comes into the public consciousness, it stays there. It can morph and evolve into something else, and it can take very many tangents from its original purpose, but once conscious, always conscious.

This was a point Dr. Carl Jung made, when he was talking about bringing psychic realities into consciousness. He observed that by the end of the 19th Century, Christianity had relegated Satan to a scary fairy tale, rather than the manifestation of Evil in the world. But after the two world wars produced their bloody results, there could be no denying that Satan visited death and destruction upon mankind, and had very nearly won. What would our lives be like today, if Nazi Germany, Mussolini's Italy, and Imperial Japan had won World War II?

No one with half a brain would doubt today that the forces of Evil in the world can and do manipulate huge masses of men and women to commit the most violent and repulsive atrocities, including Americans. Yet if you had spoken with someone a century ago, and suggested what would happen in the 20th Century, they would have told you to see a psychiatrist. By 1919, many were coming to see Dr. Jung, and he knew from then on that World War II was inevitable.

Still, the point is that we know quite consciously today that Evil does exist in the hearts of all men and women. Here I am not talking about the little sins one might confess in a Catholic Church. No, I am talking about the big industrial grade Evil that can lead to genocide.

The problem we have in our current political debate is that the parties seem to want to argue the same tired issues year after year. The talking heads of our cable channels have become Sumo wrestlers, who put on more and more weight to crush their opponents, while their opposition does the same. Both try to win by their undeniable bloated power. If you can imagine how ten 5-year-olds in the ring could influence the outcome of a Sumo match, you have some idea of what the average citizen can do. And, the powers that be want you to have that impression.

So where is the possibility that "the little guy" can really change anything? The answer comes by gaining popularity for a different brand of wrestling. For the moment we'll call it Judo. Instead of trying to influence the Sumo match, political activists need to see themselves as black belts in Judo. They can be quick and agile behind the scenes, and on unnoticed social networks, where sea changes can occur in the political ideas of the masses before the political powers know what's happening.

Just imagine what Hosni Mubarak, the dictator of Egypt, must have thought about the possibility that Facebook™ could somehow have a catalytic affect on his fate. Many of the rest of us have been caught by surprise by the influence the Internet has had on our lives in the past three decades. I can tell stories all evening about how it has fundamentally changed my life and my way of thinking about the world.

In 1985 I met my wife online. That was ten years before practically anyone even knew there would be such a thing as the World Wide Web, and Dustin Moskovitz and Mark Zuckerberg, the founders of Facebook™, were not yet born. We became among the first five couples in the world to meet online and marry. Indeed, we might be the first couple, because I've never heard of anyone who met online and married before us.
So my point is that there are ways to make changes, which no one has ever imagined. Those need to be discovered and implemented. Forget about wasting your time watching the likes of Chris Matthews or Bill O'Reilly. They are the Sumo wrestlers. Leave them to your parents, who haven't

had the spark of a fresh idea since you were born. They need the hypnotic comfort of hearing people restate positions they support night after night.

But if you are going to change the world, then change it! Introduce a new style of wrestling like no one has ever imagined. Don't worry, the nice thing about the talking heads is that they will still be there pushing the same old bar of soap when you have made your plans. At least you know where they are!

Sumo wrestlers are surprisingly poorly adapted to deal with the ideas and changes you can introduce. This is why so many of them were dumb founded when the Occupy Wall Street movement got going in earnest in the United States. They didn't even know how to think about what was happening.

Oh yes, they pulled out the usual tear gas and dogs, and they made people shut up for a time.   But did any of the discontent go away? Not on your life! Those seething wounds on a myriad of topics still simmer beneath the surface of the oppressed. If shown a way, they will rise to the occasion.

Take "flash mobs" for an example of how ideas can be communicated. They can be exceptionally effective, and they can make their point in 3-5 minutes. They can be videotaped, and live forever on YouTube. A clever and/or funny "flash mob" can go viral and pass an idea to 10 million viewers in a few days, even if it's performed only once and then evaporates instantaneously and forever.

This video can be found on Youtube as "Recycling a bottle, flashmob"

The Sumo wrestlers may ignore you, but what can they do? With their bloated size and circumscribed ring, they can do little besides keep you off of their programs. But if you've spread your idea to 10 million viewers in a few days, why would you care what's happening in the Sumo ring?

Chapter 6. Hypnosis in American Politics

Conservative Republicans will not believe Bill O'Reilly and Sean Hannity have hypnotized them. Liberal Democrats will not believe Chris Matthews and Keith Olbermann have hypnotized them. Nonetheless, that is exactly what has happened.

Do you remember that wonderful concept known as shock and awe? That's exactly the way hypnosis works! It creates a state of confusion and overwhelms our critical discernment. Both political parties simply use keywords to achieve this. They make us believe they're talking about something important, but they're really distracting us from paying attention to the issues that are truly important to our wellbeing.

Conservative favorites are abortion, family values, and socialist. Liberal favorites are fairness, gay rights, and racism. Each of these words or phrases is anchored in the depths of our psyches by years of careful and intentional repetition and conditioning. When they are used, our subconscious delivers up exactly what our original feeling was about such words, much as we regain the same feeling we had way back when listening to a favorite old song.

Many of us turn on the television every night and hear at least an hour of dutiful redelivery of these words; just to be sure we keep the feel-good trance going. But, while we've been asleep (and I don't mean literal sleep), distracted by the trance inducing words, the Masters of the Universe have been allowed to steal the values in our homes, our life's savings, and the very American freedoms that most of us hold dear.

In politics, they make you feel that the less consequential issues they are discussing are important, while they proceed to rob us of our life's savings and make us slaves to debt. This is nothing new, but it is part and parcel to how the American people have given up being Middle Class in the past 3 decades.

So what's the antidote? How do we protect ourselves? First of all we have to come out of the trance at least one time, and see it for what it is. Many of us will want to stay in the cozy place (psychologically), because we don't want to give up our cherished notions about abortion, for example, regardless of which side of the debate we find ourselves.

It does not matter that making abortion illegal once again would save zero babies. We readily allow the talking heads to talk about the issue ad nauseum rather than face the fact that the debate is meaningless. While they're talking about that, they are not talking about how the Middle Class is being destroyed by Wall Street investment bankers, which is much more significant to the happiness and well-being of the American people.

Chapter 7: Man 男

It might interest you to know that in about the 1960s Japanese researchers were working with a man, who had had a stroke, and lost the use of the right side of his brain. As a result, he could no longer read the Kanji (Chinese pictorial) characters of the Japanese language, but he could read the Kana (phonetic) characters, which are used for foreign words and to express tense and other generic ideas. This started to show that Japanese and Chinese understand language in an entirely different way from westerners. An example is the word for man (Japanese "otoko"), which is written like this: .

In various tests, hundreds of which I've carried out personally, when asked in which direction this man is going, 90% of Japanese say to the left, while 90% of westerners say to the right. The top part of this character is a rice field, and the bottom part is strength, represented by a fighter feet collected under his weight, with his feet ready to lash out at an enemy. So, for a Japanese, this image means "strength in a rice field," while westerners think of leaning into adversity or forging ahead, so our bias is for the rightward movement. This very interesting article seems to be referring to the same sense of a difference in understanding language.

I have told this story many times. It was told April 25, 2014 in response to an article a friend shared with me: Petroglyph's Rock Art or Rock Writing?

I tell this story as an illustration of how different nationalities perceive language entirely differently.

Chapter 8: Intellect v. Instinct and
Our Global Neurosis – Territoriality

*"The rupture between faith and knowledge is a symptom of the **split consciousness,** which is so characteristic of the mental disorder of our day. It is as if two different persons were making statements about the same thing, each from his own point of view ... If for 'person' we substitute 'modern society,' it is evident that the latter is suffering from a mental dissociation, i.e. a **neurotic disturbance.** In view of this, it **does not help matters at all if one party pulls obstinately to the right and the other to the left. This is what happens in every neurotic psyche,** to its own deep distress, and it is just this distress that brings the patient to the analyst."* Dr. Carl G. Jung, "The Undiscovered Self," Civilization in Transition, Volume 10 of the Collected Works of C.G. Jung, P. 285-6.

Adaptation is a desirable solution to any neurosis. *As Dr. C.G. Jung pointed out to us, many neuroses are not "cured" per se, but rather outgrown. We learn to live with the neurotic split, because we have moved on to a new way of being in the world. The medieval Catholic Church, for example, had certain ways of thinking about things, but when Galileo put his eye to the telescope and Martin Luther meditated on his conscience adaptations in perspective were inevitable.*

Many of these adaptations came after damnable and bloody confrontations. Galileo was tried and convicted of heresy while many Protestants were burned at the stake. Dr. Jung would have said that the idea that the Sun orbited the Earth was instinctual myth making, which is common to mankind since we ate the fruit from the tree of knowledge. The problem is that when knowledge shows our instincts to be wrong, humans must adapt.

We have always instinctively had to explain our surroundings and adapt to the realities of living. Only when things changed in the outside world did we have to reorient and adapt anew. But we can never deny our instincts, which provide us with the energy for life. As Dr. Jung had it:

"They cannot simply be replaced by a new rational configuration, for this would be molded too much by the outward situation, and not enough by man's biological needs." Ibid., P. 284.

The instinct of territoriality we carry in our very blood. If white blood cells sense an intruder in our body, they attack it unmercifully. This is a highly effective instinct at the cellular level, and sometimes it is even too effective. In my personal case, I have developed an allergy to beef, pork, and lamb, three meats I have eaten all of my life. According to researchers at the University of Virginia, a protein gained from the bite of a lowly Lone Star Tick has changed my fundamental biology in such a way that my body now thinks these three meats are my enemy.

Anthropologists tell us that humanity lived in matriarchal societies until about 5,000 years ago. In a time when there were few humans on Earth, there was little need for territoriality in society at large. People simply farmed or hunted in the regions where they were born.

But as things became more crowded, one group began to claim the territory of another, and territorial wars became the adaptation of the day. Societies adapted to be more patriarchal in order to survive. Over time, those adaptations led to means to identify friends and enemies based on skin color, attire, and even ways of speaking. Sikh men, for example, wear beards and turbans to this day, because in earlier times they were ways to identify one another in a battle.

Today we require a new and different adaptation. Common sense tells us that our planet is in the process of becoming overcrowded, and instinctively territoriality becomes an even more significant priority. But with globalization, dividing the planet based on race or national origin is no longer a viable long-term solution.

Human beings need to adapt new ways of living together in order to survive into the long-term future. Failure to do so can easily end us. Our rationality has both helped us develop the means of our own destruction and tells us that the adaptation is essential, but our instincts still rebel.

What will it take to cause our instincts to evolve? Japanese feudal development is an interesting microcosm of the ebb and flow of territoriality and adaptation. Human beings instinctively have learned to cooperate with one another for survival. Prior to 1600, Japanese had gradually formed into 264 feudal estates. Sometimes they battled back and forth for territory, and sometimes they cooperated.

By 1600, while the Daimyo still existed, they had joined into two major alliances—one in the east and one in the west. These two ultimately fought for territory at the *Battle of Sekigahara* , which was the largest hand-to-hand combat battle in the history of the world. Legend says 40,000 men were killed.

Even at Sekigahara, though, the seeds of the next major adaptations were planted. Will Adams (fictionalized in James Clavell's Shogun (The Asian Saga Chronology)) had landed in Japan six months before the decisive battle, delivering into the hands of Tokugawa Ieyasu 500 muskets and 19 cannons. These made the difference in the battle. Thereafter, Ieyasu consolidated his power and ushered in a 268-year period of relative peace among the Daimyo known as the Tokugawa Shogunate , while keeping the country essentially closed to the outside world.

It was only with the arrival of Commodore Perry in 1853 that the balance of adaptation began to shift with the introduction of different ideas from those found in the relatively isolated Japan. Those new adaptations ultimately led to the clash of civilizations we now call World War II, which in turn led to the Japanese denunciation of international warfare in the Japanese Constitution . Will it take chemical, biological or nuclear warfare for the rest of us to adapt to the idea that we must live in peace on a global basis? Will we survive as a species? You be the judge!

Chapter 9: Guarantor of World Order

"The gigantic catastrophes that threaten us today are not elemental happenings of a physical or biological order, but psychic events. To a quite terrifying degree we are threatened by wars and revolutions, which are nothing other than psychic epidemics. At any moment several millions of human beings may be smitten with a new madness, and then we shall have another world war or devastating revolution. Instead of being at the mercy of wild beasts, earthquakes, landslides and inundations, modern man is battered by the elemental forces of his own psyche. This is the World Power that vastly exceeds all other powers on earth. ...

"...It is not for nothing that our age cries out for the redeemer personality, for the one who can emancipate himself from the grip of the collective and save at least his own soul, who lights a beacon of hope for others, proclaiming that here is at least one man who has succeeded in extricating himself from that fatal identity with the group psyche. For the group, because of its unconsciousness, has no freedom of choice, and so psychic activity runs on in it like an uncontrolled force of nature. There is thus set going a chain reaction that comes to a stop only in catastrophe. The people always long for a hero, a slayer of dragons, when they feel the danger of psychic forces; hence the cry for personality." Dr. Carl G. Jung, "Epilogue to 'Essays on Contemporary Events'," 1946, Volume 10 of Collected Works of C.G. Jung, pp. 235-6.

As I have listened to the drums of war over the past few weeks, I can't help thinking over and over again about the 1962 Cuban Missile Crisis, and the steady hand of President John F. Kennedy in bringing the matter to a peaceful end. One can only hope that behind the scenes of President Barack Obama's pull back from the brink of an immediate military strike on Syria is a broad variety of negotiations to bring the Syrian Civil War to a peaceful end.

In some ways it seems a madness to suggest that Chemical Weapons are somehow different from all of the other perfectly adequate ways of killing an enemy, but they surely are. Chemical and biological weapons, along with nuclear weapons, have the possibility of not only subduing an enemy, but of destroying human life on our fragile planet. It is for this reason that Syrian President Bashar al-Assad has passed all bounds of human intellect, and must suffer the consequences.

There are no good outcomes to conflict in the Middle East. The Syrians attacked can light off Iran and Hezbollah, and Russia can come to the aid of Mr. Assad. Israel and Saudi Arabia are within range of thousands of rockets, as are American ships in the Arabian Gulf and the Mediterranean Sea. I could go on and on to discuss the scores of interlocking interests that crisscross the region.

We can only hope that President Obama keeps his cool head, and balances the need to stop the spread and use of chemical weapons against what can lead to something much more ugly. When Archduke Franz Ferdinand was assassinated in Sarajevo on June 28, 1914, no one thought that relatively insignificant event would lead to the millions of deaths and the poison gas of World War I, but it did only six weeks later. Relationships in the Middle East are even more complicated than those found in Europe in 1914.

Speaking for myself, I am very happy that President Obama has been able to extricate his mind from the psychic epidemic often promoted by those of our leaders who always want to "go to guns." Dr. Jung pointed out in a famous television interview, "The world hangs by a thin thread, and that is the psyche of man." His colleague Marie-Louise von Franz also commented that mankind has the potential of self-destruction:

This video can be found on Youtube as "Carl Jung: "The world hangs on a thin thread..."

CNN Commentator Fouad Ajami, a Senior Fellow at Stanford University's Hoover Institution said a startling thing on the air on September 1, 2013. He said that the United States is the "guarantor of world order." For years I have heard friends overseas refer to the United States as "the policeman of the world," but I never took that idea seriously. Most Americans would just as soon stay at home and watch a football game on television. But this is not the American that is projected on Facebook and Twitter from afar.

The great disappointment heard from the Syrian opposition when President Barack Obama didn't rain cruise missiles down on Bashar al-Assad is indicative of expectations that have risen in the world thanks to the breakdown of cultural barriers by social media. In some sense, many of my foreign friends feel that they are in a global society, of which the United States is an exemplar.

But the reality is that much work must be done before most of humanity has joined a global society, which prides itself on the idea of live and let live. Americans know that our vigorous public debate is a source of our strength, not a weakness of our leaders. By fully discussing every issue down to its base, we are able to make the best decisions for our future, without throwing our loyal opposition into jail. This is the power of the 1st Amendment to The Constitution of the United States.

If humanity is going to have a great expectation of one man or a powerful nation, then it is best to understand what that expectation can reasonably be. It seems to me that we have proven over the last decade that the United States cannot be "the policeman of the world." We are hopelessly inept in that role, as the messes in Iraq and Afghanistan have proven.

Every society must face its own internal conflicts, without having the United States call them to order in some sort of super national way. Only when these internal issues are thoroughly hashed out, will everyone be able to live in peace.

My first American ancestors came to the New World to escape religious warfare, and saw to it that we didn't make religion the basis of our government, because of the abuses that often means for minorities. Other peoples were sheltered from those decisions for centuries, but now they too must face the facts within their own societies, without a command from the top. This is the only way consensus can be achieved. If there is no consensus, then there is unrest in the body politic, which inevitably leads to bloodshed at some point. We see that on our television sets
every day.

But, the use of chemical weapons takes the issues for humanity to a new order of magnitude and importance, and I am happy that we have a leader who carries the beacon of hope to his fellow world leaders. We need a slayer of the dragons of the psyche, who can offer a candle in the darkness, and guide all of us to give one another the benefit of the doubt and rise above the psychic epidemic of the day.

We cannot allow humanity to begin its devolution toward mass extinction thanks to the machinations of a psychopath. Does this necessarily mean that the United States must commence military action against Syria, with unpredictable results? I think the answer to that question depends upon what happens in St. Petersburg this week, and not what happens on Capitol Hill. I'm very happy that President Barack Obama is our man on the scene for that discussion.

Chapter 10: Tyranny Is Tyranny Whether It Comes in Red Coats or Blue Pin Stripes

We must stand against tyranny in every generation! Liberty is never finally won!

On August 27, 1776 The 1st Maryland Regiment stood strong for Liberty at The Battle of Brooklyn, saving General Washington's Army from annihilation! They were among the first combat deaths of the U.S. Army! Only 9 made it back to American lines with their Major. 256 lie in an unmarked common grave under the streets of Brooklyn, New York. In 1869, the stand of **"The Maryland Line"** was called **"more precious to liberty than any other moment in history."** Long may their story be told! "The Immortals" is a description that "The Maryland 400" rightfully earned. To this day, Maryland is referred to as "The Old Line State" thanks to the courage of Marylanders during the American Revolution.

Why did they fight so hard and willingly die for liberty? The back story is significant! When Henry VIII wanted to have more wives, he cut off the Pope and founded the Church of England. Many notable Britons opposed him, including the Speaker of the House of Commons, St. Thomas More, who lost his head over the controversy. These events were part and parcel of the religious wars between Catholics and Protestants, which raged in Europe after Martin Luther nailed his Ninety-Five Theses to the door of All Saints' Church in Wittenberg, Saxony in 1517.

By 1634, King James I was tired of the carnage, and gave his Catholic subjects the Colony of Maryland, because they were persona non grata in England. Over the next century and a half many Catholics established what is today the State of Maryland. But the story went on despite James I's best intentions. Anglicans began to come to Maryland too, and many Catholics were forced to move to the northern and western regions of Maryland, where the 1st Maryland Regiment was recruited for the Continental Army.

The men of The Maryland Line were sons and grandsons of those Catholic forefathers, who had been pushed out of England, and then pushed away from the bounteous Chesapeake Bay. When they saw the Red Coats coming, they knew they had to make a stand. This far and no farther! And there, at the Old Stone House in Brooklyn, they gave their lives to preserve the liberty their recent ancestors had found in North America.

My fellow Americans of the 21st Century are complacent about our liberty. Just as the Anglicans seeped into the Catholic Colony of Maryland, and kept pushing Catholics out, tyranny morphs and finds its way to subjugate humanity. Few Marylanders could tell you whether their ancestors fought on the side of the Revolution or the side of the Crown in the American Revolution. All that has washed away by time. But those loyalists to tyranny who stayed must have changed their tune after 1783, and we wouldn't know who their descendants are today.

But tyranny we can recognize, and today it comes in blue pin stripes, and is headquartered on Wall Street. There venal investment bankers concoct the most convoluted schemes to separate the rest of us from our life's savings. Since 2008, they have pulled off the biggest public theft in the history of history.

One of their number, Henry Paulson, who was Secretary of the Treasury under President George W. Bush, persuaded the Congress to give him overwhelming authority to save his "too big to fail" colleagues from financial collapse. On one notorious evening he gave 9 banks $25 billion each on the strength of a single piece of paper signed by each Chairman. That was $225 billion dollars given to 9 banks on 9 separate pieces of paper. The audacity of it boggles the mind; and was intended to do so!

The settlements of the U.S. Justice Department with Citigroup and Bank of America, $9 billion and $17 billion respectively, are chump change by comparison. Records or not, they are only being accepted to give us the illusion that something has been done about Wall Street abuses. What happened to the rest of us is part of the point. The banks had no losses from our mortgages. Their risks were all covered by mortgage insurance and credit default swaps, so when mortgages went bad because the economy collapsed from profligate risk taking by Wall Street, they were alright.

It is a fundamental principle of the law that if you have no damages, you cannot recover in a law suit. This principle was famously explored in Leon Uris's best selling novel, QBVII. If our politicians were really looking out for the People of the United States, they would have remembered that doctrine and saved average citizens from the loss of their life's savings. But that is not what they did!

Instead, they allowed the banking community to exploit the situation. When Americans lost their jobs and ability to pay on their mortgages, our politicians allowed them to foreclose, thereby harvesting the life's savings of many millions of Americans.

Did you ever wonder why the banks could stay profitable and pay their officers $100 million annual bonuses? This is why! They were getting paid double on our mortgages. Their losses in the 2008 financial crash were covered almost immediately by President Bush's bailout, with the so called TARP program adding over $700 billion to our National Debt. We, the American People and our children will be paying for that bailout for decades.

Then the bankers blamed the catastrophe on individual Americans, who had no way of knowing that the bankers had added risk on risk to the financial system for at least two decades, until finally it could not support the weight. When Americans lost their jobs and their cash flow, they felt it was their fault they could not pay, and they turned over their homes to the banks!

What a scam! I can just imagine the conversations they've had on Wall Street. "Wow! That was profitable!
How long do you think we have to wait before we can do it again?!"

That's the point! If we don't wake up and do something about it, the venal bankers who have foisted this abominable fraud on the American People will do it again to our children, and this time they'll do it intentionally.

This attitude was summed up by a 1%er, who I happened to be standing next to at a conference on September 15, 2008, the day the collapse of the financial system became undeniable. We had been watching the sobering news on television, and he said to one of his friends, "It was silly of us to have a financial crash in the middle of a Presidential campaign." I guess next time they'll do it with better planning!

It is time for the American People to wake up to what has been done to us and our children! Tyranny is tyranny, whether it comes in Red Coats or blue pin stripe suits. They will do it again to our children if we don't draw a line in the sand now and say, "This far and no farther!"

Chapter 11: Revolutionary Spirit of the Age

"It was the best of times, it was the worst of times, it was the age of wisdom, it was the age of foolishness, it was the epoch of belief, it was the epoch of incredulity, it was the season of Light, it was the season of Darkness, it was the spring of hope, it was the winter of despair..."

So it was that Charles Dickens opened his epic novel, A Tale of Two Cities (1859). He was writing, as Victor Hugo was three years later in Les Misérables (1862), about a revolutionary time, which saw the American Revolution followed quickly by the French Revolution. It was a time when the people finally said, "Enough!" to the Oligarchy, and rose up against their oppressors.

They were writing at another revolutionary time, just before and during The American Civil War, when the American southern states were being forced to change their views on the operation of their economy, which was manned by slaves. Both men's home countries, Britain and France, were being called upon to take sides in the American struggle.

As is true of all great artists, they found a way to talk about the issues of their day by addressing them in the unconscious psyches of their audiences. Perhaps they were not even doing this intentionally. They were writing decades before Sigmund Freud and Carl Jung began exploring the workings of the psyche. But like all good artists, they were expressing something that was pushing on them from within.

I didn't get it at first; that recent and forthcoming movies have been expressing the fact that the collective unconscious of humanity is in a new revolutionary age. I didn't even bother to see Les Misérables (2012) when it came out in the theatres, but I plan to see it now. The people of Turkey have shown us quite explicitly that this 150 year old projection of Victor Hugo still applies to us today by singing their own version of "Do You Hear the People Sing?" in Gezi Park, and by putting together a music video that hits us over the head with the analogies, which need no longer be metaphorical.

These videos can be found on Youtube as "Les Mis "Do You Hear The People Sing," and "Do You Hear the People Sing? – Turkey"

Dr. Carl G. Jung wrote of "The Spirit of the Age", and knew that when this spirit rises, individuals alone can do precious little to change things until the collective unconscious morphs into something else. He reported that he knew from 1919 that World War II would come, and that it would be ugly once again, because he saw it in the dreams and visions of his private patients. In response to a letter from Mrs. Alice Lewisohn Crowley, who wrote him asking what she could do in her situation, he wrote:

I beg you to consider your life. If they are going to send you to Poland, you only can suicide yourself. Please forgive this crudeness! It is my anxiety for your life, which makes me say such things. Remember, I warned you before America went to war. It is urgent that you do something and quick! Europe is in a desperate situation. I am sorry and I am helpless.

Yours affectionately, C.G. Jung
[Source: Maxwell Purrington of Carl Jung Depth Psychology page on Facebook™]

It was the courageous Bulgarians, with their # ДАНСwithme rebellion, who put this in the context of the age-old struggle between the Oligarchy and the average person for me. This is their third revolution, since 1989, but each time the people rise up and select new leaders, and the new leaders fall back into the old patterns of corruption and the New Feudalism. The Egyptians saw this with the Arab Spring, and they will be showing how they feel about it again on June 30, 2013 with their #Tamarod Petition. The Bosnians are responding too, with their #jmbg demonstrations scheduled for July 1, 2013, and hundreds of thousands of Brazilians have already been at it for a couple of weeks with their #ChangeBrazil campaign.

Even I was swept up in the #OccupyWallSt demonstrations, which began September 17, 2011, and who can forget the violent and repressive actions of police forces across the United States, proving #TheBigLie to our Rights of Freedom of Assembly and Freedom to Petition Government for a Redress of Grievances. You don't have to call someone a king to know when you're being treated like a feudal serf.

Millions of the Baby Boom generation lost their life's savings as a result of the profligate behavior allowed on Wall Street, but our media continues to whistle in the wind, saying the economy is getting better; that home sales are getting better. Yes, that may be true as a statistic, because our population is much larger and is in need of housing, but those of us who lost big because Wall Street was allowed to pile risk on risk aren't getting our life's savings back, and that is the operative fact in this discussion about the Spirit of the Age.

As I reported a few days ago, "Elysium" and other apocalyptic movies we are projecting on screens all over the United States are simply reflections of the collective unconscious. We would not pay to see these movies, if they did not contain a message our psyches need to bring into consciousness. Do you think "Elysium" will be allowed a long theatre run? Whisper who dares!

This video can be found on Youtube as "Elysium – Official HD Trailer"

Competing forces of Oligarchy and the rest of us un-people are always present, but they have gotten seriously out of balance around the world once again, just like 1776, 1789, 1861, 1914, 1929, 1939-45, 2008, and yes, in Turkey, Brazil, Egypt, Bosnia and the United States of America today. I am not saying we can do anything about it. Like Dr. Jung in his response to Ms. Crowley, I think we are all helpless to change the inevitable. I am simply an observer, and this is my observation. Perhaps it will give you a different lens through which to observe the events that are unfolding this summer.

I can offer only one piece of advice to our brothers and sisters, who are coming out onto the streets this summer. Keep your demonstrations non-violent. Violence gives the Oligarchs an excuse to violently repress you. Assume that if someone is using violence, he is probably an *agent provocateur* sent by your local Oligarchs to create an excuse to force you back into your homes, with bloody bodies and damaged lungs. It is far better to simply leave a demonstration that has become violent, and live to demonstrate another day in another way. A five-minute flash mob videotaped, posted and viral on YouTube is far more effective than a pile of bloodied citizens rolled over by tanks and hidden from the public by penguin documentaries.

Chapter 12: What Do They Want? Wall Street, Oakland, Istanbul, Sao Paulo

The pot boils over around the world! There is an old story that asks, "How do you boil a frog?" The answer is that you put the frog into a pot of cool water, and then let the heat rise slowly until the frog is boiled. If you raise the heat too quickly, the frog jumps out.

This is a worthy metaphor for the discontent that has given rise to major demonstrations around the world since the Arab Spring, and promises to continue everywhere. For the last decade, Turkish Prime Minister Recep Tayyip Erdoğan has proven to be an expert chef with a Frog Soup specialty, gradually turning up the heat with his Islamist agenda. But, as the Turkish demonstrations have clearly shown, his violent repression of the Gezi Park protest has turned up the heat too much on the Turkish People, and they are jumping out of the pot.

But the Turkish phenomenon is only the latest manifestation of nagging discontent that has been simmering in the unconscious of the Middle Class everywhere. The wealthy have been derisive of the demonstrations, often claiming that they are marginal groups with unclear agendas, but in sum, they represent discontent with the economic conditions that have been foisted on people around the world by the wealthy. **The chief features of this discontent have been wealth inequality, political corruption, and corporate influence of government.**

"Elysium", the new movie with Jodie Foster and Matt Damon, projects the consequences of allowing the wealthy to continue to raise the heat on all of us, which they have been doing for over forty years. This is what happens when we allow The New Feudalism to overwhelm us.

This video can be found on Youtube as "Elysium – Official HD Trailer"

On August 23, 1971, Lewis F. Powell, Jr. (later appointed Justice of the U.S. Supreme Court) sent a memorandum to the Chairman of the U.S. Chamber of Commerce entitled "Attack on the American Free Enterprise System". That memorandum broadly described how the elite could advance their interests in ways that would not be broadly noticed, but would gradually hollow out the "American dream".

The Savings & Loan crisis of the early 1990s was an early manifestation of the risks of these behaviors, but the Wall Street Financial Crisis of 2008 was a more poignant demonstration. Because they had been so successful since the Powell memo, Wall Street was able to duck the consequences with their "too big to fail" claim, while blaming a single mother of two with a mortgage in Memphis for the crisis.

The real reason for the crisis was that without controls on Wall Street, which had been removed with the repeal of the Glass-Steagall Act controlling certain banking activities, investment bankers had been allowed to add risk upon risk until the system crashed. They were able to pay themselves $100 million bonuses because they were so smart in creating "financial products" out of air. They have continued to pay themselves these huge bonuses since, because they were so smart in making the average American pay for their greed run amuck. Fraud was rampant throughout the mortgage syndication system, but practically no one has been held accountable.

The elite 1% of the wealthy sold us a bill of goods when they convinced us that what was good for them would be good for the rest of us because of the "trickle down" phenomenon—if they were living high, they would hire the rest of us to do their dirty work, in a kind of New Feudalism.

The trouble is there is no "trickle down" anymore. The majority of the money produced on Wall Street stays in financial instruments, which investment bankers can manipulate like a gambling casino. Since they control the stakes and the rules of the game, it is far more profitable to fleece unsuspecting investors from around the world than invest in the infrastructure of the United States.

The demonstrations we are seeing play out across the world are saying just one thing quite emphatically. Enough!

Chapter 13: There Will Be Blood

"You already feel the fist of the iron one on your back. This is the beginning of the way. If blood, fire, and the cry of distress fill this world, then you will recognize yourself in your acts: Drink your fill of the bloody atrocities of the war, feast upon the killing and destruction, then your eyes will open, you will see that you yourselves are the bearers of such fruit. You are on the way if you will all this. Willing creates blindness, and blindness leads to the way. Should we will error? You should not, but you do will that error which you take for the best truth, as men have always done." The Red Book by C.G. Jung, P. 254; Reader's Edition P. 203.

I noticed the blood during my first reading of The Red Book, but I did not comprehend its prophetic significance until I read Lament of the Dead: Psychology after Jung's Red Book. Fundamentally, what Dr. Jung was telling us is that we are "lived by the dead," in the sense that the dead need our blood in order to play out the significance of the lives that went before.

Bundled into the fundamental idea is the sense that every culture calcifies, and it is only by blood that major change occurs. We can see many examples in recent history and current events. Psychiatrist Carl Jung learned from his own experiences that one can even predict when blood will be spilled. During Christmas night 1913 [eight months before the outbreak of World War I] he had a vision:

"I saw something terrible and incomprehensible ... I saw the peasant's boot, the sign of the horrors of the peasant war, of murdering incendiaries and of bloody cruelty. I knew to interpret this sign for myself as nothing but the fact that something bloody and dreadful lay before us. I saw the foot of a giant that crushed a whole city. How could I interpret this sign otherwise? I saw that the way to self-sacrifice began here. They will all become enraptured by these tremendous experiences, and in their blindness will want to understand them as outer events. It is an inner happening ...

"May the frightfulness become so great that it can turn men's eyes inward, so that their will no longer

No one can doubt that the blood of World Wars I and II caused the German and Japanese peoples to change how they address the rest of the world. This was not because they were subdued by all of the deaths, but rather because those who survived had no choice but to look inward for their strength, and when they did they found something different from what they had been sold by their leaders before and during the wars, based on the cultures in place at the time.

Dr. Martin Luther King, Jr. knew from his own vision, which he described the night before his murder that change would come to the racial situation in the United States only when a blood sacrifice was made. While our racial relations are certainly not where many of us would hope them to be 50 years after the "March on Washington" and his famous "I Have a Dream" speech, they are certainly vastly different from where they were before that August afternoon in 1963.

This video can be found on Youtube as "MLK's Last Speech,"

As we look at many of the huge political controversies facing humanity, we can see that major change comes with blood. Many of us would like to see a change in our American attitude toward gun violence in our country. We know that the blood sacrifice of 26 innocents in Newtown, Connecticut last December was not enough to change the calcified attitudes of members of the National Rifle Association.

Dr. Jung explains why we have not seen more political change around gun control since the Newtown tragedy thusly:

> *"The masses as we know follow the law of their own inertia and seek, if disturbed, to restore the state of balance as speedily as possible, no matter how uncomfortable it may be."* C.G. Jung's Commentary on Keyserling's La Revolution Mondiale (*May 13, 1934*)
>
> [*Collected Works, Civilization in Transition, Volume 10, P. 498*].

Unfortunately, we must conclude that only when enough blood is shed, and the horrors have truly overwhelmed our sensibilities, only then will we see the changes so many of us yearn to see.

Looking out into the world today, we see many calcified attitudes, and much blood being shed. We can only hope that these many unfortunate killings will lead to significant introspection on all sides, which will once again lead us to an age of peaceful tolerance of one another.

One can easily see how we are lived by our dead from the actions of "The Virginia Flaggers," who are still posting Confederate flags along the I-95 corridor, to "restore the honor" of the Confederate Dead, 150 years after The Civil War. Presumably none of these people favors a reinstitution of slavery in this country, but the battle cries of old don't die easily. When I was a boy in Norfolk, Virginia, The Virginian Pilot newspaper daily published little coupons throughout saying, "Save your confederate money, the South shall rise again."

I have often wondered why there is not more about Dr. Jung's activity during the war years. Perhaps it was because he knew the contents of the German soul from his many therapy clients, and he knew that wouldn't be changed without blood, since that is the only way to change the collective unconscious.

It is not a question of arguing my point. Ask yourself, what political changes do we seek requiring blood before the changes we seek will be implemented? Here's a short list: abortion rights; gay rights; tighter gun restrictions; women's rights; and stricter penalties for driving while intoxicated.

In Japan there is zero tolerance for drunk driving. If you are caught with anything over zero liquor on your breath while driving, you lose your driver's license for life. We used to kill about 25,000 on our roads every year because of drunk driving. Now, thanks to Mothers Against Drunk Driving (MADD) forcing legislatures to act, that has improved, but we are still killing about 13,000 per year by drunk driving. To get to the level Japan achieved, more blood will be necessary—regrettably.

In 2007, I published a book called Tsunami of Blood. I imagined that if I sounded a warning about what I saw as a very bloody age, perhaps it could be averted. Dr. Jung has now explained to me through The Red Book why it couldn't. But now, with millions of people dead in the Middle East and Afghanistan, we see rifts emerge among the inhabitants themselves. Those rifts could only emerge when enough blood was spilled. Only then could women shout into the ears of their warrior husbands, "Enough!"

Osama bin Laden viscerally knew that if he took down the World Trade Center, in a very bloody way, change would happen. He thought many would rally to his banner. And he was right! They did! But what also happened is that calcified ideas in the deep unconscious of his original sympathizers began to break apart, and that has caused blood feuds centuries old to be reignited between brothers. Rather than getting all of Islam rallying to his flag, he got himself and millions of his fellow travelers killed, not to mention the innocents of those lands.

It's not a pretty prescription, and I point it out with a heavy heart. But it is clear that Dr. Jung was onto something when he started to encounter blood in The Red Book. Now it is for us to find ways to avoid spilling more and more innocent blood. Can we do it? Unfortunately, There Will Be Blood!

Chapter 14: Meltem Arikan, Bully Politicians and the Presence of Justice

Meltem Arikan has been nominated for the Freedom of Expression Awards 2014 of the Index on CensorshipTM. This essay supports her nomination and describes what Meltem experienced in 2013, which goes far beyond traditional censorship. Abusive attacks on prominent performance artists, up to and including threats on Meltem's life, were to stifle dissent and artistic freedom in the entire Turkish arts community.

"True peace is not merely the absence of tension: it is the presence of justice."
The Rev. Dr. Martin Luther King, Jr.

Meltem Arikan knows censorship. She experienced that in 2004. What she experienced in 2013 was far more culturally dangerous, rising to the level of intentional persecution and repression of dissent entirely. Censorship implies the rule of law is at least operational in a society. Meltem did not have the benefit of the rule of law in her native Turkey in 2013. Meltem's 4th novel, *Yeter Tenimi Acıtmayın (Stop Hurting My Flesh)*, was banned in early 2004 by the Committee to Protect the Minors from Obscene Publications, with the accusation of "writing about the non-existing incest fact in Turkey, attempting to disturb the Turkish family order with a feminist approach." The ban was lifted after a two-month legal process. Subsequently, the Turkish Publishers' Association awarded Arikan the "Freedom of Thought and Speech Award 2004." That was back when the rule of law and modern civilization still held sway in Turkey. Differences of opinion surely existed, but at least one could take a dispute to court and seek a rational judgment.

What Playwright Meltem Arikan experienced in 2013 was far worse. She has had to leave her home country to save her life, because politicians stirred up a psychic epidemic, a witch-hunt, against her and the main creative team of her play, *Mi Minör*. What ensued was much more than the persecution of an individual writer, resulting in her choosing to leave her country to save her life. It stifled dissent, especially artistic dissent, throughout Turkey.

It is justice and the rule of law that Turkey has lost since 2004, when Meltem battled her country's censors. If the issue is only censorship, at least rational and educated people can ultimately make the right decision. Even a loss along the way can ultimately lead to a better society. But Turkish politicians now resort to the logic of the mob to serve as their censors. As Dr. King also famously said,

"The arc of history is long, but it bends toward justice."

Regrettably, the arc of history in Turkey has been bent backward, toward a stifled society. Such societies can become more and more repressive for a time, as the 20th and 21st centuries have clearly shown, but ultimately they fail, as Nazi Germany and the Union of Soviet Socialist Republics ("USSR") proved on a grand scale.

It is the role of artists to challenge the status quo, knowing that only by breaking old intransigent attitudes can new attitudes emerge to improve life for all. Meltem Arikan's play *Mi Minör* accomplished that with creativity, spontaneity from her audience, and joy. It included the audience in music and dancing, letting the audience experience their interactions with their own attitudes, and thereby forging changes in perspective.

I will first give you a sense of the story of her play, and then describe what happened to strip Meltem of her rights. *Mi Minör* is set in a dystopian society, with many ham handed regulations, none of which are actually regulations of an existing government, at least not to my knowledge. Meltem and her collaborators had fun developing somewhat whimsical and nonsensical regulations, from banning the treble keys on all pianos, the source of the play's name, to forbidding women to eat ice cream cones. The venue for the play is comparable to an ice hockey rink or other indoor sports arena. When the audience arrives for the play, they learn that they are to be the citizens of a fictitious country, based on the mathematical function Pi (π). The fictitious country of Pinima has a population of 3,142,857, an area of 314.285 km2, and national borders in constant change, with the Pinish language spoken by most. Its elevation is 3.14 meters above sea level. The audience has the option of sitting in the bleachers or participating in the action on the floor of the arena, which becomes "Pinima Square."

The government of the country is a "deMOCKracy." But there is little justice present. One of the two lead characters, The President, makes all the decisions, which means he never sleeps. He runs for office under the imprimatur of both major parties. There are no other candidates allowed, even for the cosmetic purposes we have them in the United States, and he siphons the wealth of the country away in hollowed out gourds, the country's major agricultural export.

Mi Minör has a unique and innovative extra feature in that every performance becomes a global social networking adventure. The audience is invited to bring and use cameras, smart phones, notebooks, and laptops, and Wi-Fi is provided to the house. The play sports a live twitter feed under the rubric #MiMinor, which is projected on the wall of the arena.

The problem arises in Pinima when The Pianist, a lowly street pianist, who is the other lead actor, is stopped from her Pinima Square performance, and police tape is put over the treble keys of her piano, because, she is told, they sound too much like a woman screaming. The Pianist gets more and more angry, as various rights are taken away, until she begins to promote demonstrations against the government's edicts. She broadcasts all of the events in Pinima Square to everyone in the world through her smart phone using Ustream™. Digital actors, the audience, and anyone in the world with access to Twitter™ or Facebook™ can interact with the live performance.

Over the 25-performance run of *Mi Minör*, more than 10,000 people attended the live venue in Istanbul, from December 1, 2012 to April 14, 2013. Even more remarkable, more than 17,000 people from 27 countries as far away as Mongolia participated in one or more of the performances live. The play was frequently "TT" ("top Tweet") in Turkey during its performance, including during its premier, and it even reached the top 10 of global Tweets for one remarkable 15 second period.

The two lead actors were interviewed many times on Turkish television, including CNNTurk, in long comprehensive conversations. Nothing was hidden from the authorities. No one complained. Permissions were taken from the governorships of each of the three venues where the play was performed.

It was only after the play closed that the witch-hunt began.

About May 28, 2013, a peaceful demonstration began to save the few remaining trees in downtown Istanbul at Gezi Park, adjacent to Taksim Square. The government over reacted, with violent repression of the demonstrators. Meltem attended some of this demonstration as a private citizen, but was not one of its organizers. As the situation escalated over the next few days, more violence was used, and the world community began to bring pressure on the government to calm things down. That's when the government used the "oldest trick in the book," diverting attention from their growing embarrassment before the world community. As part of a concentrated propaganda campaign beginning June 1, 2013 several officials and their political party functionaries denounced Meltem Arikan, blaming her and members of the creative team for causing the Gezi Park demonstrations.

They asserted *Mi Minör* was intended by Meltem Arikan and members of the main creative team as a rehearsal for the Gezi Park demonstrations, and amounted to an attempted coup d'état against the Government of Turkey. This allegation was preposterous to anyone who attended the play or followed the bloodshed and violence perpetrated by the Turkish authorities, but tens of thousands of people at various government rallies and in television audiences knew no better than the narrative of the authorities. Because of the attacks on a popular play like *Mi Minör*, the attacks had a chilling effect on the entire arts community.

Throughout this period there were negative social network hash tag campaigns, and threats to Meltem's life and to the lives of the main creative team began to emerge from the general public, with emotions instigated by all of these artifices. All of them felt they had to leave the country for their own security.

The result of these events is that artistic expression has been severely repressed in Turkey as a whole. What should we call it? Was it censorship of the entire artistic community of Turkey, in effect? Or is it persecution and repression by the functionaries of a sitting government?

I will be the first to acknowledge that we have bully politicians in the United States too. Governor Chris Christie of New Jersey is a case in point in our current political cycle. But, in his case, the United States Attorney is investigating allegations of abuse of power, and he may find his way to jail. God knows several of the recent governors of our State of Illinois are sharing prison meals for their misconduct in office, and on January 21, 2014, former Governor Bob McDonald of Virginia and his wife were indicted for accepting bribes. Who will set things right in Turkey and return the rule of law? Even censorship by a legally appointed authority would be better than living in a country where injustice prevails, and the government maintains its power by the rule of the mob.

Chapter 15: I am Guilty! I am a Provocateur!

I am guilty! I am a *provocateur*! Since some Turks seem to have labeled me thusly [Note: Read from paragraph 6 below], I might as well wear it proudly!

Hell, I can't be late for breakfast in the morning without provoking my wife! I never title or write an essay without intending to provoke my reader to think about what is happening in the world and about how they feel about it. I almost never do anything in business without trying to provoke a reaction.

I am guilty! I am a *provocateur*! The Archetype in Action Organization™, which I founded, has always had as its mission to provoke people to think about their Rights, and their methods in achieving those Rights. We have always focused on Human Rights, Women's Rights, and Prevention of Human Trafficking.

If we don't publish articles on our focus issues, we always try to provoke people to study the works of Dr. Carl G. Jung, whose work was dismissed in his lifetime, perhaps because people were afraid of their own psyches. Today it is uncommon to find Jungian analysts, but they exist everywhere. Part of the reason may be that health insurance has insisted that mental health professionals medicate their clients instead of helping them find happiness.

Dr. Jung's work was largely about helping people find their true place in life, whatever that may be. He said, "Bring me a normal man, and I will fix him for you." His point was that we are all "normalized" by our society (forced to conform in various ways), but normality is not the same as happiness. He was a *provocateur* too!

Today Dr. Jung's work is really more useful to artists and activists than it ever was in the therapist's office, although it is useful there too. I founded the Archetype in Action Organization™ in order to convey this fact to as many others as possible. I am guilty! I am a *provocateur*!

Over a five-month period between mid-November 2012 and mid-April 2013, I participated in a play in Turkey called "*Mi Minör*". I did this by participating on a Twitter™ feed from wherever I happened to be, which was projected on the wall of the theatre in Istanbul. The play is about a fictitious dystopian society, which has heinous and repressive regulations and behaviors of its government, **none of which are regulations of an existing government in the world,** at least so far as I am aware.

I have a good imagination, but never in my wildest thoughts did I think this play would threaten any existing government. I believe it was attended my many Turkish officials over its 5 month run, and so far as I know, no one ever objected. Considering how many people attended the play, I'm sure a relatively complete list of those officials who attended the play could be produced if that would be useful. It was discussed in long comprehensive interviews on CNNTurk and other television channels in Turkey, and so far as I know, no one ever objected to its production, though its content was widely discussed.

Recently a number of Turks have insinuated that I might be an agent *provocateur* of the United States government. To those people I say, "Get a grip!" [NOTE: "Get a grip" is an American English colloquialism suggesting that in my opinion you might need professional therapy with a licensed psychologist.]

To suggest that a play about ice cream cones and piano keys can undermine a government, suggests to me that you might be trying to create a mass hysteria, like the Salem Witch Trials in the United States, in order to divert attention from something else. What could that be? Whisper who dares! What is it you are trying to hide by such diverting theatrics? Why would the United States government do such a thing when its support of your Prime Minister is widely known? The logic escapes me.

To those who still think I am an agent *provocateur* I say, yes, I am in my business life and my avocation of promoting the works of Dr. Carl G. Jung. In my business life, I maintained the largest private data circuit between the United States and India during 1995-96. That circuit supported businesses in medical transcription, medical billing, typesetting for the printing industry, and the first private call center in India with U.S. dial tone. This effort began in 1994. You will speak to very few Indians today who know of my input or were in these Indian businesses before me.

It was a 7/24/365 circuit between my office in the United States and Chennai, Tamil Nadu, India. Like an airline that has to pay for its seats, whether full or empty, I had to find ways to fill this $50,000 per month circuit, and build the businesses in India that would make it profitable. I built a similar circuit to Rawalpindi, Pakistan.

In 1998, I made four speeches in India about the efficacy of doing medical transcription in India for U.S. hospitals. [Note: The first time I mentioned this idea to a Director of Medical Records in the United States, she couldn't stop laughing at me. When she finally caught her breath, she spoke to me as if I was talking about Mars.] My company was trying to find eight companies in India, which would produce our business. Within 18 months, 640 companies had started by Indian entrepreneurs, who thought they could get their Indian-American-doctor brothers, uncles, and cousins to work with them. Some of them succeeded, and some didn't.

In the process, I was instrumental in building what is now the largest medical transcription company in the world. Before I retired from the company, we had established 40 production centers in India employing 6,000 Indian medical transcriptionists. The industry now employs well over 25,000 Indians.

I am guilty! I am a *provocateur*! I wonder how many lives I made better by my work? An official of the Republic of India once told me that every job created supports 10 Indians, because they need butchers, bakers, and candlestick makers to support them.

In my lifetime I have lived in Japan for eight years, and started businesses in the United States of America, Japan, Korea, India, Pakistan, and several countries in the Middle East. I have been to India 43 times since 1994, and to the Kingdom of Saudi Arabia 23 times since 2002, always supporting the healthcare industry in these countries and the United States, not to mention many other travels.

While building a company in Japan between 1979 and 1984 I literally flew around the world 15 times, and had business connections in Korea, Germany, Belgium, France, Italy, Saudi Arabia, Iraq, Indonesia, and Libya, to name just a few—oh, yes, and in the United States in New York, Tennessee, Michigan, and Texas. I speak Japanese and Mandarin Chinese, with a smattering of French.

It is surely true that no American can leave our borders without being suspected of being an agent of the U.S. government, with the possible exception of tourists confined to buses and cruise ships.

To the Turks who have accused me of being such a government agent I say, "You'll never know for sure." How does one answer that accusation? In any case, it's nearly impossible to prove a negative, but, if I say "yes" you can either believe me or not, perhaps thinking that I am somehow trying to puff myself up. If I say "no" you can either believe me or think that I am keeping some deep dark secret.

I have been to Turkey exactly three times in my lifetime, for a total of 7 days. I have always loved the country. I have not often thought very much about the Turkish government, except to wonder what it is doing about healthcare information technology.

In 1996, I visited the usual sights in Istanbul for two days, staying at a one-star hotel near Topkapi Palace. I ate alone at a sidewalk café one night, and came to a time when I had a call of nature, so went into the café basement to the men's room. While I was there, I realized that my wallet with my passport was missing from my pocket. I scrambled up the stairs and out the door, and received my wallet passed to me like an American football by the Maitre D' as I ran through the door. I don't know if I would ever see it again if the same thing happened in my country. My betting is not.

In February 2013, I came again and stayed with my friend, Memet Ali Alabora. I performed my role in "Mi Minör" in the theatre on February 10, 2013. We had a lot of laughs about the satire in which we were performing. I never heard a word about the Turkish government.

Once again, in early May 2013, I visited Memet Ali's home for a relaxing weekend after a grueling week of attending the Health Information Management Systems Society Middle East conference in Riyadh, Saudi Arabia (HIMSS ME 2013). We watched the movie "Flight", we visited a teashop, I was included in a karaoke evening, and I did some work, which included printing out a document related to my company on Memet Ali's printer. None of this involved Turkish politics in any way.

I am very proud of and honored by my friendship with Memet Ali Alabora, not to mention all of my other Turkish friends. These draw me to want to bring business to Turkey, as I have to many other countries during my long career.

To those of you who still think my involvement in a theatrical event somehow damns me, I say you are just being silly. Indeed, in retrospect this witch-hunt will seem just as bad as the regrettable McCarthy Era in the United States. I recall during my high school years we read and discussed "The Crucible" in my English class, presumably because my teachers in the U.S. Navy high school I attended in Yokohama, Japan wanted us all to know how mass hysteria can seize a community. It is about the Salem Witch Trials, and was written as an artistic allegory for McCarthyism. I urge you to read it.

Is this the kind of Turkey you want? Is this the kind of Turkey you are promoting? Is this how you welcome visitors and encourage foreign businessmen to bring their ideas and investments into Turkey? Is this how you seek membership in the European Union?
Maybe it's time for "The Crucible" to be produced in Turkish. I'll bet a lot of people would come to see it. Would a 60-year-old play about a shameful chapter in American history be banned in Turkey? No worries, it's probably time for it to have a new run in either New York or London. God knows we have had plenty of people trying to stir up mass hysteria in my country over the past decade. Think of the publicity angle! "Banned in Istanbul!" I can think of some candidates to play the leading roles either way.

"More than once it has been said, too, that the Salem witchcraft was the rock on which the theocracy shattered." Is this why the American Founding Fathers, a century later, insisted on absolute Freedom of Religion in our Constitution of the United States? Was it to protect us as humans from our own tendency toward mass hysteria? I don't know. What do you think?

So far as I know, every foreigner who crosses a border into another country has opinions. I have many. So far as I know, I am one of over 1 billion bloggers in the world. Do you propose to defame all of those with whom you disagree? That seems like a big job!

I'm guilty! I am a *provocateur*! To quote a dear friend of mine,

> "*I'm guilty! I choose to rebel in order to exist.*
> *I confess, whatever you do, I will continue to say no to violence and show passive resistance and answer your unbalanced violence with my intellect and pen!*"

Chapter 16: Making Gold in Turkey

"The meeting of two personalities is like the contact of two chemical substances: if there is any reaction, both are transformed.
Dr. Carl G. Jung

Prime Minister Recep Tayyip Erdoğan needs to take a lesson from Dr. Carl G. Jung. You see Dr. Jung's long study of Alchemy is often misunderstood, but Mr. Erdoğan is in the process of getting a demonstration of what Dr. Jung was talking about when he wrote all of those books about Alchemy.

Most people think that Alchemy is about making gold. Well, that is partially true, but it is the metaphorical gold that is created in the human psyche and spirit, and in human societies. It relates to finding the perfect state of the human spirit. But as the alchemists knew, it can often require acid to reach the gold. The Turkish People are currently tasting that acid.

The ancient alchemists, who really served as early psychologists, were often under threat of death for saying anything that brought into question prevailing religious doctrine. As a result, they created their own language of metaphor and chemistry; but often what they were really talking about was psychology. They knew that when things change, or you meet a new person, your whole relationship to the world can change.

The "container" of an alchemical process is called a vas, or cauldron, but in this case we are talking about the cauldron of the human psyche, the psyche of a group, or in the case of recent events in Turkey, the psyche of a nation.

One of my mentors used to tell me that whenever you take someone out of a group, or add someone in, the group changes. This is the type of thing that Dr. Jung was talking about when he was talking about Alchemy, though most people were not intuitive enough to get what he meant. Indeed, he was called a mystic or worse to suppress his ideas, when the reality was that he was a professional scientist, who was exploring new scientific information that challenged the wisdom of the day.

Most outsiders cannot understand why the Turks are so upset about Gezi Park, which includes a small stand of trees in the center of Istanbul. They say the Prime Minister has made things better for all Turks, so why not just let him keep on doing what he's doing?

Actress Pınar Öğün summed up the response quite succinctly in this interview with Al Jazeera English. When asked about all of the successes for Turkey of the Erdoğan government, she said, "Well, we have our points too." Her point is that Mr. Erdoğan and his government have lost touch with the feelings of average Turks on too many issues to name.

Mr. Erdoğan's state violence in the name of order offended most Turks, and most people of common decency around the world. Now many Turks, who were unconscious of their myriad gripes against the government, which have been building up in many ways for years, have had the new chemical, excessive use of tear gas and violence, thrown into the alchemical vas of the nation. We Americans have seen similar excesses of violence in our own country in the past year, and we have not forgotten.

This video can be found on Youtube as "Chapulation Song - We'll be Watching You,"

Behavior such as that is bound to have an opposite reaction, which quite simply leaves the reason for the original demonstration for Gezi Park in the dust. Dr. Jung would explain that the Prime Minister had constellated an archetype in the psyche of the nation. A great American general summarized it more graphically in this way:

"When you put your hand into a bunch of goo that a moment before was your best friend's face, you'll know what to do." General George S. Patton.

You can suppress the psychic reaction, but it will never go away, and like a pressure cooker without a safety valve it can come out in unimaginable ways. As lawyers are given to say about an objectionable comment in a trial, "You cannot un-ring a bell." This is the mistake that most authoritarian rulers have made over the centuries.

There is good news, but it can take a long time to germinate:

"*When I despair, I remember that all through history the way of truth and love has always won. There have been tyrants and murderers and for a time they seem invincible but in the end, they always fall - think of it, always.*" Mohandas K. Gandhi

This is the gold of which Dr. Jung and the alchemists spoke.

Chapter 17: Superman, Standing Man and Gezi Park

A trip to your local movie theatre these days is terrifying, especially if you know something about the work of Dr. Carl G. Jung. Standing in the lobby last weekend I was shocked to have the assortment of choices presented on graphic posters. Why am I so concerned? The vast majority of choices covered either apocalypse ["World War Z" and "White House Down"] or superheroes fighting larger than life enemies ["Man of Steel", "Wolverine 2", "The Lone Ranger", "Elysium", and "The Hunger Games: Catching Fire"].

In the Introduction to The Red Book, Sonu Shamdasani points out the following"

> "In the years directly preceding the outbreak of war, apocalyptic imagery was widespread in European arts and literature. For example, in 1912, Wassily Kandinsky wrote of a coming universal catastrophe. From 1912 to 1914, Ludwig Meidner painted a series of works known as the apocalyptic landscapes, with scenes of destroyed cities, corpses, and turmoil. Prophecy was in the air." [The Red Book, P. 199, Reader's Edition P. 18]

The point is that the arts project the contents of the collective unconscious, and often predict world events in unexpected ways. Turkish Prime Minister Recep Tayyip Erdoğan recently blamed 112 artists for causing the 2013 demonstrations across Turkey, but as Dr. Jung showed us over his long life of prodigious scholarship, art only shows us what is in the unconscious of all of us, including the artists.

It just happens that successful artists are somehow more sensitive to the psyche, and serve as channels to connect us to our inner selves, whether they know this or not. No one would go to see "Man of Steel" if we did not have a deep unconscious need to see a superhero vanquish a seemingly intractable enemy. Who is that enemy? Whisper who dares! Whoever and whatever it is, the sad fact is that Superman is not coming. We have to serve as our own superheroes.

Nowhere have the powers of the collective unconscious and the power of the heroism of a single human being been more graphically demonstrated than in Istanbul on June 17, 2013. Choreographer Erdem Gündüz went out into the center of Taksim Square and simply stood quietly, saying absolutely nothing, for eight hours. He was quickly called #DuranAdam on Twitter, #StandingMan, and within hours his silent vigil was being replicated all over the world. He was surely channeling something in the collective unconscious of his countrymen and perhaps in all of us.

Within 24 hours, the Turkish government was moving to make standing silently illegal in Turkey. What flashes in my mind is Walt Disney's cartoon movie "Fantasia" of 1940, which includes the famous scene of "The Sorcerer's Apprentice". Mickey Mouse [Recep Tayyip Erdoğan] finds that he can regiment the brooms [AKP] to do his bidding. But, he is quickly overwhelmed because the brooms [Turkish People] have a different idea of how they will behave. It takes a superhero, the sorcerer, to stop the chaos. **Who or what will that superhero be in Turkey?**

Turkey's traditional answer was the Army, but Mr. Erdoğan has jailed many Army leaders, and, as the Egyptians learned to their dismay, the Army cannot always be trusted to have the interests of the common man and woman at heart. As I said above, Superman is not coming, so the Turkish people will have to restore order and then make the changes they want themselves.

Dr. Jung spent most of the rest of his life elaborating on the significance of the dreams and visions he had beginning in 1913. There were many of these, but one in particular was noteworthy to show the significance of projections of the unconscious mind, which we often now see in the movie theater, on television, on the stage, in music videos, and in every other kind of artistic work.

> "It happened in October of the year 1913 as I was leaving alone for a journey, that during the day I was suddenly overcome in broad daylight by a vision: I saw a terrible flood that covered all the northern and low-lying lands between the North Sea and the Alps. It reached from England up to Russia, and from the coast of the North Sea right up to the Alps. I saw yellow waves, swimming rubble, and the death of countless thousands." [The Red Book, P. 231; Reader's Edition, P. 123.]

Two weeks later the vision repeated, and then again twice in June 1914 and once in July 1914. The murder of Archduke Franz Ferdinand took place on June 28, 1914, and the hostilities in World War I began with the guns of August [historically chronicled in The Guns of August by Barbara Tuchman in 1962].

In my own small way, I know that prescient visions are real, and are served up by the unconscious. When I am driving on the highway, whenever I have a vision of a police car come to mind I slow down. Invariably, within 2 miles I will see a real police speed trap. I don't need a radar detector for this, because unconscious clues in the environment tell me it is true. Perhaps the oncoming traffic changes its speed imperceptibly, or perhaps they flash their lights. I'm not sure what clues my unconscious notices, but I do know these visions work with flawless accuracy.

I feel confident that Erdem **Gündüz** did not really know nor did he predict what would happen as a result of his silent vigil. But, as a choreographer and artist, he knew that he could channel something in the unconscious of his audience. Within 24 hours it is likely that 25% of all human beings on the planet found that something in their own unconscious and understood its power.

I am sobered to notice that one of the movies mentioned above opens on June 28, 2013. It's probably nothing, but I find myself staring at that last sentence with dread.

Chapter 18: Where Is Darth Vader When We Need Him?

*"Only an infantile person can pretend that evil is not at work everywhere, and the more unconscious he is, the more the devil drives him. It is just because of this inner connection with the black side of things that it is so incredibly easy for the mass man to commit the most appalling crimes without thinking. **Only ruthless self-knowledge on the widest scale, which sees good and evil in correct perspective and can weigh up the motives of human action, offers some guarantee that the end-result will not turn out too badly.**"* Dr. Carl G. Jung, Aion, ¶ 255

Thank God for the writers of Blacklist and Scandal, who have started to offer us nuanced characters with complex personalities, which are not only good or bad. We have slowly begun to move away from the "Star Wars" generation, when Darth Vader was the evil doer, who was out there and the hero and the princess were pure good.

In the past century, movies and television have assumed the role of the myths and fairytales of the Middle Ages and before. Dr. Carl Jung explained that the role of stories has always been to

"Give expression to unconscious processes, and their retelling causes these processes to come alive again and be recollected, thereby re-establishing the connection between conscious and unconscious." Id., ¶ 280

Movie makers have long understood the relationship between our archetypes and their success at the box office. But one problem has emerged in that most of the stories they tell set up the hero as an initially weak but at bottom fundamentally good person, while the "bad guy" is always dark and evil from the outset. That is not how our psyche works.

When the evil Darth Vader is projected outside of us, we can sleep better having seen the movie, believing that the evil is over there in some other dark being. But we know that evil lurks in the hearts of even those who project themselves as paragons of good from some of the dark chapters of the fundamentalist Christian churches. Jim Bakker and Ted Haggard are sordid cases in point. Even so, many Christians simply ignore the possibilities of evil intent, and go right on throwing money at celebrity pastors, with very little attention paid to their accounting practices and personal behavior.

We have the habit of seeing "dark side" style incidents as outside ourselves; as not us. We love to see the incessant chatter about the sexual proclivities of people like Bill Clinton and Anthony Weiner, because we can see ourselves as "good" in comparison. Indeed, sexual scandal has turned our mainstream media into pale copies of Jerry Springer and Maury Povich, rather than any longer making any pretense of providing us with news, which may make a difference to us, like the war in Syria.

All of us have within us both good and evil in relatively equal measure. But our movies and television programs go ahead and let us project our evil natures upon someone else. Finally, in Blacklist and Scandal, and a handful of other worthy offerings, we are starting to see characters who demonstrate the dualities of their personalities.

Dr. Jung's point was that we need to become conscious of the fact that evil lurks within each of us, in order to properly decide what we want in our society and what we do not. He had a ringside seat on the emergence of The Third Reich, living in neutral German speaking Switzerland throughout his life. He saw how Adolph Hitler was able to turn the resentment of normal Germans into a race of barbarian murderers. They were on the losing end of the World War I killing machine, and wanted retribution for their losses.

Two years after World War II, my own father was walking along a road in Bremerhaven, Germany, when a truck containing a few German workmen passed him and knocked him unconscious with a board. Apparently they felt, correctly, that they could get away with their assault. My father was unconscious for three days. And yet, I have little doubt that those men went on to live relatively normal lives thereafter, and the memory of what they had done probably submerged into their unconscious and they were able to put on a good front for their wives and children.

Years later, when I was 15, I was lost late at night in a rural city in Japan. I was certainly apprehensive at 2:00 a.m. in an unknown city, in a country that had produced murderous fanatics only a generation before. It was very dark! But, a taxi driver picked me up and drove me two hours to my home, arriving there about 4:30 a.m. I could easily have gone missing that night, but that man had decided, as most of his countrymen had, that the sort of behavior my father experienced was not what they wanted in their society.

Everyone, who has served in battle, knows that there are certain parts of our psyches that contain dark things. The reason most families say something like, "Dad never talked about the war," is precisely because we don't want to go there. The truth is, though, it is not only warriors who have such dark places.

Anyone who has ever lost a boy or girlfriend to a rival knows such dark places. While jealousy arises as a motive in murder only in extreme cases, we all do know that there are some things that can "push our buttons," and get us into a fury--sometimes uncontrollably. Still, we are able to live in society, because we normally control those impulses, and acting on the fury is the rare exception rather than the rule.

In our normal lives we do "weigh up the motives of human action," and common sense prevails. Most of us live moral lives. And yet, we know, that there are certain scenarios that can cause a different result. This is why stories, which show people weighing the moral alternatives we all face are useful in helping us know ourselves. The trouble with Darth Vader is he gave us the crutch of thinking that evil is outside, and can be fought with a light saber. As Neo learned in "The Matrix,"

> *"One doesn't become enlightened*
> *by imagining figures of light,*
> *but by making the darkness conscious.*
> *The latter is disagreeable and therefore unpopular."*
> Dr. Carl G. Jung

Throughout the world there are people who do not see Americans as always "the good guys," as is the common perception of Americans about our country and its motives in the world. There are many reasons for that, which are beyond the scope of this essay. I might like to suggest that we understand these issues, but Dr. Jung would first advise the aphorism, which appeared on the Temple of Apollo at Delphi:

"Know thyself."

Chapter 19: What Karma Taught Me About Alchemy

"Unbroken Wholeness in Constant Flowing Motion"
This is how Physicist David Bohm answered when asked to describe reality.

"Karma" is my standard collie. His messages to me are quite simple, and they fall on the dualistic continuum between physical and spiritual needs, though for "Karma" they always begin with the physical. Perhaps that's how all living beings began to get what they needed. They started on the physical end of the spectrum, and gradually, as they evolved, found their way toward a spiritual communion.

Usually, when I am sitting in front of the television, "Karma" comes and punches me in the knee, letting me know he wants one of two things—food or out. It's pretty easy to guess which it is because Karma's first priority is always food. He deals with me like a human Pez™ machine; punch Dad's knee and a morsel of something he likes will appear. Once he has the treat, though, his psyche moves along the continuum from pure want to satisfy his hunger to the spiritual end.

He is very precise about the ritual of his dinner, which somehow evokes the spiritual side of the process. He wants his dinner in the middle of the living room, so that he can circle it, but he doesn't begin the circling until my wife and I (his herd) are settled in our chairs. Then he circles and plops down with his front paws encircling the bowl. He eats with his eyes closed, like he is being transported into another dimension. It is clearly a communion for him.

The Chinese concept of Yin-Yang symbolizes this process, because no matter how many white swooshes that exist in the universe, there are always complimentary black swooshes with white swooshes inside them. The circle symbolizes the alchemical vas cauldron), where ingredients are mixed until there is a balance of the various infinite number of pairs of opposites.

The opposites are essential to all life, because between them exists the energy that powers our lives, for better or for worse. But it is not only one continuum, but an infinite number.

Dr. Carl Jung showed us the way when he spoke of introvert-extrovert, sensing-intuitive, and thinking-feeling, and he did think that Yin-Yang symbolized the mixture of these opposites. But he also knew that pairs of opposites exist in infinite quantity, size, and levels of the psyche. It is for this reason that he took up the study of medieval alchemy, which sought the metaphorical "gold" and goal of human life—what Buddhists call "Enlightenment"; what the Taoists called "The Way"; the "Heaven" of the Christians, Muslims, and Jews; and the "Realized" nature of any adept.

When "Karma" wants out, he punches me in the knee. When I get up from my chair he heads for the stairs to the door, rather than the kitchen. The need is obvious, but as his photograph shows, once he has taken care of the immediate, he moves across the physical-spiritual continuum to appreciate the wind blowing through his fur.

In the evening he will lie in front of our home, watching the garage door of our neighbors, where two border collies live. It isn't that they are such great friends, they barely acknowledge one another when they are together, but it seems he has a spiritual need to see other beings like himself, even if very briefly. And perhaps it is true that it is the waiting that is the spiritual communion, and not the reality.

All sentient beings turn to the sun, even trees and flowers. Yes, there is the physical need of the photosynthesis, but who can doubt that a leaf or a flower petal turning to the sun is also a spiritual celebration of its existence. So it is with all of us. While there may be human beings who do not like or must protect themselves from the direct rays of the sun, these are surely exceptions, like the Yin-Yang symbols within the Yin-Yang symbols, and even they seek to become their opposite.

Each of us, each of our families, our communities, our countries, our religions, and our planet are alchemical cauldrons. We put into each many different ingredients over a lifetime, and what we perceive in our world are the precise and perfect results of our mixture. Have you included the best ingredients you could offer today?

The Big Lie

Chapter 20: The Big Lie in American Politics

The American Republican Party has taken "The Big Lie" as a political concept to new heights of mendacity. Adolph Hitler defined the political stratagem of "The Big Lie" in Mein Kampf:

> "...in the big lie there is always a certain force of credibility; because the broad masses ... more readily fall victims to the big lie than the small lie, since they themselves often tell small lies in little matters but would be ashamed to resort to large-scale falsehoods. It would never come into   their heads to fabricate colossal untruths, and they would not believe that others could have the impudence to distort the truth so infamously."

Hitler's propaganda chief, Joseph Goebbels, used the artifice of blaming his enemy, the British, for "The Big Lie" in order to hide his own. He said in "From Churchill's Lie Factory," dated January 12, 1941, "The English follow the principle that when one lies, one should lie big, and stick to it. They keep up their lies, even at the risk of looking ridiculous." Certainly Conservatives have accused Liberals of big lies recently so in fairness the reader should know that I have no plans to vote for another Republican in my lifetime. You may therefore consider the source as you read my list of the 10 Big Lies Republicans are telling the American people.

Big Lie #1: Lower Taxes Create Jobs. Under President George W. Bush, businesses and wealthy Americans enjoyed the lowest taxes in a century, and yet only 1.1 million jobs were created in that 8-year period, as compared to 22.7 million created during President Bill Clinton's term, before the tax reduction. Furthermore, President Bush was credited with the loss of 1.55 million jobs in his last 3 months in office, and that momentum carried over to the loss of 1.83 million jobs during the first 3 months of President Obama's Administration. Republicans must admit that President Obama was handed a collapsing economy.

Big Lie #2: Republicans Reduce the Deficit and National Debt. Statistics clearly show that the last Republican President to reduce the National Debt as a percent of Gross Domestic Product ("GDP") was Richard Nixon, not someone we usually associate with fiscal concerns. President George W. Bush increased the National Debt from 56.4% to 84.6% of the GDP, about $6.1 Trillion in round numbers. Even though saddled with President Bush's vastly increased debt service, President Obama has only increased the debt by $1.7 Trillion, while faced with saving the American economy from total collapse. Every Democrat since Roosevelt has reduced the National Debt as a percent of GDP, while every Republican except Eisenhower and Nixon has increased the debt.

Big Lie #3: Lower Taxes Help New Businesses Create Jobs. This is Republican bologna of the first order. New businesses never have taxes, because in their startup period they are spending more money than they're earning. Furthermore, since they usually suffer losses during a startup period of at least 2-3 years, they have "tax loss carry forward" in later tax years. Therefore, taxes rarely enter into any decisions relating to creating new businesses.

Big Lie #4: Social Security and Medicare Will Go Bankrupt. No they will not, because the solution is simple. Everyone earning under $106,800 pays Social Security tax on 100% of his or her income. If you earn more than $106,800, you pay nothing on the amount over that amount. This means that someone earning $1 Million per year pays less than 1% of their income for Social Security. How is it fair to have such regressive taxes? The wealthy take the most from our society in the form of assets we all buy: they have roads for their trucks, armies to defend them, and education for their employees, among many other benefits that most of us pay for but use very sparingly. Secondly, our population has grown more than 50% since the end of the "Baby Boom", so while that generation is larger, the population paying taxes to cover their benefits is also growing very fast. Republicans, who have already arranged for less than 1% of our population to control more than 50% of our national wealth, are just hoping to take even more, and create a society of slaves to debt. Some would say they have already succeeded!

Big Lie #5: Republicans Believe in "Family Values". Well, perhaps they do, but the ones they use in politics are just diversions to keep Americans from talking about how the wealthy are ripping off the country and most of us. Here's their list:

a) **Abortion:** Prohibiting abortion will save exactly zero babies. Before abortion became legal in the United States, about 16% of our medical community was regularly committing felonies by performing illegal abortions. Did criminalizing our medical community help the nation? How about those well meaning sorority sisters with their coat hangers? Was that better? How many places in the world can someone go to get an abortion today? If we criminalize abortions again, babies will not be saved, we'll go back to the bad old days, and we'll further brutalize our society once again.

b) **Gay Rights:** What business is it of ours to even think about what our neighbors do in the privacy of their bedrooms? Do you live in a glass house? Why are we even talking about this? Do we think we will stop the behavior by making it more difficult for our fellow countrymen to live their lives? What are Conservative Republicans thinking? I think they're just using the usual smoke and mirrors to hide the fact that they are destroying our future.

c) **Evolution:** Conservative Republicans support fundamentalists who want us to believe that humans were developed by "intelligent design" 5,000 years ago. They need to stop supporting militant ignorance. We have remains of human ancestors dating back 4 million years, and we can see back to within 500,000 years of the "Big Bang" and down to particles smaller than atoms. Why are we militantly and ignorantly denying science? Is this the way to make the United States of America the envy of the world again? I recently heard a news story saying that a fundamentalist Christian was mad at a teacher for revealing to an 11-year-old girl that the "tooth fairy" does not exist. What are they thinking? How will children raised in those environments cope with our steadily more complex real world?

Big Lie #6: Barack Obama Is Responsible for the "Obama Economy". George W. Bush handed President Obama a collapsing economy caused by the profligacy of his Wall Street supporters. As the #OccupyWallStreet movement is beginning to show, Americans aren't buying the Republican game any more. Most of us remember President Bush and his cronies doling out nearly $1 Trillion in TARP (read "stimulus" or "bailout") before they left office. The Republican Party needs to change its obstructionist behavior to something that makes sense for the average American, or it can forget the Presidency for the next generation.

Big Lie #7: "Obama Care" Is Bad? Well, it's an interesting buzz word the Republicans are using to hide the fact that before the healthcare changes passed during the Obama Administration, there were over 40 million Americans without health insurance, and many children and people with pre-existing conditions could not obtain health insurance from the Republicans' insurance company allies at any cost. Of course, the wealthy could care less about that. If you pay yourself a $100 million bonus, you don't have to worry about health insurance. It's just the rest of us, who do the work in their companies to make them wealthier, who do!

Big Lie #8: Democrats Are Soft on National Defense. So far, the Republicans are looking pretty ridiculous on this one. First they told "The Big Lie" to get us into a war in Iraq, thereby creating hundreds of millions of new enemies for us in the Middle East. Next they refused to follow the Geneva Convention, thereby proving to those new enemies that we are not the benevolent country we think and pretend we are. And now Republican candidates are implying that they want to get us into another war with Iran. Just great! Meanwhile, President Obama has shown a quiet and effective methodology for handling our foreign affairs. He's actually following a dictum espoused by a Republican President of the early Twentieth Century, Theodore Roosevelt, who said, "Speak softly, but carry a big stick." It is really not necessary to have everyone think we're the policemen of the world.

Big Lie #9: Ronald Reagan's Administration Was Good for the Economy. Ronald Reagan's performance on our National Debt was the worst of any President in history. During the Reagan Administration the National Debt increased from $930 Billion to $2.68 Trillion, an increase of 2.89 times over the level it was when he took office. The National Debt increased by 23.6% on average every year of the Reagan Presidency.

Big Lie #10: Illegal Immigration Will Be Stopped by a Republican President. Mitt Romney ran an "amnesty state" during his time as Massachusetts Governor, while Rick Perry made coming to this country more attractive by allowing illegal immigrants to pay in-state tuition at state universities. As long as we have illegal immigration, we will have an artificial slave class in the United States, because illegal immigrants are not protected by minimum wage statutes. All of the evidence over the last 3-4 decades says that neither major party will push for sensible immigration reform   .

So there you have it! Ten "Big Lies" the Republicans are telling to win the White House and control of Congress. Are we going to continue to stand for it?

Chapter 21: Response to Romney's New Hampshire Speech

Mitt Romney's words (January 10, 2012 are in quotation marks; my responses are in bold.

"Tomorrow we go back to work.

"We do remember when Barack Obama came to New Hampshire four years ago. He promised to bring people together." **And he would have but for Republican obstructionism.**

"He promised to change the broken system in Washington." **But the Republicans decided to break it even worse than it was. When will Republicans stop running for office and start collaborating with their Democratic colleagues in solving the problems of the Nation?**

"He promised to improve our Nation. Those were the days of lofty promises made by a hopeful candidate." **And he certainly has improved our country's economy, which George W. Bush left in free fall when he left office.**

"Today we're faced with the disappointing record of a failed President. The last three years have brought a lot of change, but they haven't offered much hope." **Speaking for myself, I hope the Republican stranglehold on Congress gets ended for a generation with Election 2012.**

"The Middle Class has been crushed. Nearly 24 million of our fellow Americans are still out of work, struggling to find work or have stopped looking. The median income in America has dropped 10% in the last 4 years." **All thanks to the Republican scheme to cram down the Middle Class and destroy labor rights.**

"And soldiers coming home from the front lines are now waiting in unemployment lines." **Only because your Wall Street buddies won't invest the Trillion dollars they've held aside in the hopes of defeating President Obama. They know that if they do not hold back the Democrats, their gravy train at the Pentagon will be drastically reduced. That's right! An additional $350 billion per year added to our defense budget since 2001 cannot be justified.**

"Our debt's too high, and opportunities are too few." **The debt was nearly tripled by Ronald Reagan and nearly doubled by George W. Bush. Why should we believe Republicans will reduce it. The last Republican to reduce the National Debt was Richard Nixon.**

"And this President wakes up every morning, looks out across America and is proud to announce, "It could be worse. It could be worse? That's not what it means to be an American, 'it could be worse.' Of course not!" **Aside from running negative ads against your opponents, you have said absolutely nothing about what you would do to improve things. Oh, perhaps you said you'd keep taxes low for the rich, a strategy that has proven ineffective in creating jobs over the past decade. Bill Clinton's Administration produced 22 Million jobs; George W. Bush's Administration produced a net loss of jobs, if you count the first 3 months of the Obama Administration when the economy was in free fall thanks to the Bush policies.**

"What we know as Americans is our unwavering conviction that we know it must be better and it will be better." **It will be, but not if Republicans continue to obstruct Congressional action.**

Chapter 22: The Balkanization of the Republican Party

The "sick man" of American politics, the Republican Party, has finally begun to show us just how messed up it really is. Here's my assessment of where they are in the 2012 election campaign, with separate observations for each branch of the party.

1. The Greedy Bankster Branch. The wizards of Wall Street must be quaking in their boots after the Iowa Caucuses, which proved that unlimited gobs of cash could no longer be relied upon to buy elections. Despite the fact that he spent millions upon millions of dollars defaming other candidates, their glamour boy could only manage about the same percentage of votes as he got in 2008, before he spent all of that money. Actually, this turn of events is ominous, because it suggests that the Masters of the Universe will use more insidious strategies in the future. Richard Nixon's rat fucking "plumbers" unit comes to mind.

Of course, this branch can always be relied upon to produce a certain number of votes from the greedy bastards, who have their snouts in the government trough far more than any Social Security recipient. But they seem to have been abandoned by any Republican with a sense of smell.

2. The Militantly Ignorant Tooth Fairy Branch. There has always been a branch of humanity that wanted to militantly ignore science and the facts. The Roman Catholic Church hauled Galileo up before the Inquisition for daring to say what had been known for at least two thousand years, that the Earth is not the center of the Universe. He got the last laugh though, because he knelt before them and swore on the Holy Bible that the Sun orbited the Earth. The Grand Inquisitors dutifully recorded the proceedings verbatim, thus ensuring that Galileo's Abjuration would make monkeys of them for all time.

Part of Galileo's punishment for his heresy was that he could never write about astronomy again, so he went off and wrote about quantum mechanics instead, which is the basis of what is happening at The Large Hadron Collider in Switzerland today, thanks to the Republican Congress's refusal to fund basic research in the field in the United States.

Evangelical Christians have among them the modern militantly ignorant, who deny the findings of the Hubbell Space Telescope and the most powerful electron microscopes. These tell us that there are more than 100 billion galaxies, each containing millions of stars, so if there is an "intelligent designer" of the universe, S/He must be resting someplace, because S/He sure isn't anywhere around here. Rick Santorum has cornered this branch of the party, bringing into his fold all those who refuse to tell their children that there is no Tooth Fairy, nor any Santa Claus, and the only God involved in their creation was their own passion on a hot night. I'm personally surprised we haven't heard the stork mentioned in the current election campaign, but there's still time. One wonders how they think their children will compete in a world where the Europeans, Chinese, Russians, Indians, Japanese, Brazilians and most others are teaching their children the truth about science.

Though a darling of this Tooth Fairy Branch, Michelle Bachmann has finally faced and embraced the lesson women have been stuck with since human kind expanded to the point that there was not enough land for everyone, so someone was going to fight over it. Patriarchy trumps every time!

3.   **The Angry Youth Branch.** The angry youth of the Republican Party have come to the stunning realization that it is their lives that will be bet on the wars all of the Republicans seem to want to embrace. In Iowa they don't have a vision of getting a fat job in the defense industry, so they're suspicious of their elders' choices. They're not yet independent enough to break away from their parents' dogma that they must vote Republican, but they're sure not going to vote for a hawk. Unless Ron Paul decides to run a third party candidacy, they can be relied upon to vote for President Obama in the 2012 election, once they're behind the curtain of the voting booth.

4.   **The Fat Blow Hard Branch.** Newt Gingrich's Fat Blow Hard Branch of the party hasn't yet given up on tired boilerplate. They believe his outrageous rhetoric that the Palestinians are an "invented people," as if the Americans were not.

In response to his militant rhetoric about Iran, they hop up and down and shout, "Yeah!" You'd think they were watching Alabama play Auburn, ignoring the fact that such a course would surely create even more millions of enemies than we've already manufactured over the past decade thanks to Republican imperialism.

In their heart of hearts, most Republicans do understand that neither party will fix the illegal immigration problem, because both want a below minimum wage slave class. Nonetheless, they keep signing on to the rhetoric that something will be fixed. It won't!

5. **The Marlboro Man Branch.** Like their namesake, this branch of the party is a dying breed that will be entirely finished if Rick Perry or his ilk were to win the White House. They fail to understand that it will be too expensive to maintain their Ford F-150 pickup trucks for city driving if their heroes start a war with Iran and go on with Karl Rove's imperialist designs. If the Administration of George W. Bush was the apogee of this branch of the party, it also sewed the seeds of its demise by proving that the United States cannot force Democracy in its image, nor can it be the policeman of the world. Rick Perry's laughable performance as a presidential candidate only provides us with a tragic epitaph.

6. **The Vanishing Voice of Reason Branch.** At 1% of the Iowa vote, I think we can safely say that Jon Huntsman's branch of the party is nearly completely snuffed out. Since most Americans are reasonable, it is the final and conclusive evidence that the Republican Party is finished. Of course, some untoward event could occur to raise the zombie from the grave, but the demographics of the country are against the party, regardless of what candidate becomes its standard bearer. If they win in 2012, they may be done for a generation, because the economy is not going to recover robustly no matter who sits in the White House. How would they explain that in 2016 if they won?

Chapter 23: Who Really Prints the Money

Congressman Ron Paul has made "End the Fed" a mantra this election season. But, to a very large extent, his disgust is misplaced. In this article I will discuss as simply as possible where the problems are with the U.S. Federal Reserve Bank ("Fed"), America's central bank, and point out why it cannot easily put an end to the recession we are currently navigating. The real culprits are Wall Street bankers, who have circumvented all controls and made even the mechanisms the Fed normally uses irrelevant. Wall Street bankers are now the ones with the money printing press!

Here are the typical issues related to the Fed:

1. Inflation and Deflation—Controlling the Money Supply.
Like any commodity, if there is too much money its value goes down, while if there is not enough in the system its value goes up. Whoever controls this must put enough new money into the system to cover all of the goods and services produced beyond what was produced last week or last month or last year. As we have a larger population, producing more baby cribs, we need more money in the system, just for the relative money supply for all goods and services to remain even.

Whether it's the Fed or the Treasury, someone has to be responsible for maintaining the level of the money supply. It is a "Goldilocks" issue. Put too much money into the system and you have inflation; too little and you have deflation.

2. Fractional Reserve Banking System:
Under the "Fractional Reserve" banking system, a bank only has to have in its vault a small percentage of the amount it loans out. This percentage varies depending on a number of factors. If the number is 3.33%, the bank can create nearly 30 times the amount in its vault and Federal Reserve deposits simply by making bookkeeping entries in the accounts of borrowers. If it is 10%, then

the bank can create nearly 10 times the amount in its vaults and Federal Reserve deposits. This is how the Fed typically increases or decreases the money supply based on the needs of the economy.

The problem we have right now is that the bankers who receive the freedom to loan more money have a nefarious political scheme. They do not want to lend out extra money, because if they do our economy would get going, and Democrats would win political control once again. This in turn would mean effective regulation over their casino games, which is our real problem. This is why even though the Fed is making funds available at extremely low costs, there is insufficient money going out into the economy. The only remedy for this is for the government itself to start spending money to pay salaries and suppliers, which in turn will put sufficient funds back into the hands of consumers and get the economy going again.

3. The Money Masters Video

A 1996 video entitled "The Money Masters", available on YouTube, clearly predicted that we would have a financial collapse. That video explained manipulative inflation and deflation causing booms and busts, the "fractional reserve system" and the fact that private interests control the Fed as our primary issues. They missed one key point, however. Left totally without regulation, as the Wall Street banking system was under the Administration of George W. Bush, the Money Masters were able to make the meager controls the Fed possesses irrelevant. This is the primary issue we face in 2012. The Money Masters, who dominate the Republican Party, want us to all be slaves to debt, and they want the bones they throw to the 99% to be as limited as possible, while they gather all of the real value to themselves.

In our current political situation, it really does not matter whether the money supply is controlled at the Fed or the Treasury (private v. public). Even if it were in the Treasury, the people who serve in the Treasury typically come from the private banking sector and would want to return to that sector after their government service, so they will do nothing to upset the apple cart of The Money Masters. In both cases, they have to control the money supply correctly or face insurrection. In the United States, we are lucky that our revolutions can now be at the ballot box; but if we didn't have the vote, we would find more traditional ways to express our opinions, as many have in the developing world.

At the same time, the "fractional reserve system" is simply a tool for managing money supply, so it really doesn't matter whether the tool is used by the Fed or by the Treasury.

4. The Right to Print Money
The issue really arises about who has the right to create money. With the current system, money is created through debt. The Fed pays for U.S. government bonds with credits rather than actual money, and those credits go into bank accounts. The U.S. Treasury thereby increases the "national debt". But, unless bankers loan the new money through their rights under the "fractional reserve system," nothing is added to the money supply except the amount of the original purchase, and the economy does not get going.

If, on the other hand, the Treasury simply printed its own money, separate from Federal Reserve Notes, and declared them legal tender for all debts public and private, as Abraham Lincoln did during the Civil War, no debt would be created. The government would simply pay its bills with this legal tender backed by the full faith and credit of the United States. The federal government would therefore not be at the mercy of Wall Street bankers in terms of getting the economy going once again. The Treasury could simply print the money instead of printing Treasury bonds, through which it borrows the money.

Yes, there would be an inflation risk, but the increase in goods and services would increase the need for a greater money supply, thereby solving this problem. If the Treasury took back all of the power to control the money supply from the private bankers, who own the Fed, then at least there would be some political oversight on the process.

5. Wall Street Creating Funny Money Is the Real Problem.
When we deregulated the banks in the late 1990s, we allowed Wall Street to create all kinds of sophisticated financial instruments. When Wall Street started putting mortgages into securities, we effectively allowed them to add huge amounts of risk to the system, and this led to tragedy on September 15, 2008, when the house of cards began to collapse in earnest

Here's how it worked. If a bank could create mortgages equal to 10 times the money it had in its vault, the Wall Street bankers syndicated those mortgages by buying them from the banks and putting them into securities onto which they could then apply an additional 10 to 30 times leverage. The mathematical effect of this was to increase the risk in the economy from 10:1 to 300-900:1. Even in Las Vegas, the best odds you can get on Roulette are only 35:1, so this leveraging of the syndications was a huge bonanza for the Wizards of Wall Street. No wonder they were paying themselves $100 million bonuses. They could take a bundle of mortgages worth $100 million, and make them seem like they were worth $1-3 billion (which they clearly were not).

The result of all of this was to create an artificial "money supply", because the Wall Street bankers were in fact selling those instruments of inflated value for actual cash from outside investors like oil barons and little villages in Norway. When the bubble collapsed, those were the people who were badly hurt, while the Wall Street fellows got to cry, "We're too big to fail!"

And that was only one of their many schemes. They have created a derivatives environment that is truly gargantuan. At the time of the September 15, 2008 crash, there were approximately $513 TRILLION worth of derivatives outstanding in nominal value. The estimates today, even in the face of the global recession, range from $708 trillion to $1.4 quadrillion (yes, that's 1,400 trillion). Considering the fact that the total global economy for goods and services for the entire world—all economies—is only $50-60 trillion annually, the numbers they have wrapped up in electrons on Wall Street are truly numbers beyond comprehension.

Now Wall Street critics, who read this, will immediately tell you that the "nominal value" isn't anything like the real exposure, which is only perhaps 1% of the "nominal value". The reason is that many of these derivatives would cancel one another out if there were another collapse. Even at 1% though, these risks are amazing, potentially amounting to the entire U.S. economy for 1 year. Are they nuts?!! Are we nuts for letting them get away with this?!!

6. What Election 2012 Is About

The Republican mouthpieces of Wall Street don't want to give up their gravy train. Who would? The problem is that the 99% have to live out here in the real world, where we have become slaves to debt and their profligacy. They change the rules to please themselves, and this time around they pleased themselves by creating a casino so big that even the largest central bank in the world cannot control it.

The 1% controls whether our economy prospers or not, because they control the money supply, and the volumes they are working with are far beyond anything the Fed can manipulate. This is why the Fed has stated unequivocally that it will keep its rates low until 2014. They've run out of gas for the economy unless the bankers start lending, because that's how our system works. When we print money we create debt simultaneously. If the bankers don't play along and loan the money into the economy, nothing happens.

One way to circumvent this conundrum is for the Treasury to print money instead of debt instruments (Treasury Bonds), and then use that money to pay the obligations of the United States. It would be amazing how fast our "national debt" would come down then! The Federal Government could fix our infrastructure without all of these contortions, and thereby put money back into the pockets of the average American.

This is a complicated area of the economy. In this article I have simplified discussion of some of the processes, so that the average American can understand the big picture. Obviously, any of the implied solutions will be debated for a long time, but if we don't understand where the problem really lies, we are at risk of losing our basic freedoms.

Chapter 24: 1968 and 2012

"Injustice anywhere is a threat to justice everywhere. We are caught in an inescapable network of mutuality, tied in a single garment of destiny. Whatever affects one directly affects all indirectly." Rev. Dr. Martin Luther King, Jr.

Now that we've reached 2012, I can't help my foreboding. It has nothing to do with the "end of the world" or anything like that. Rather, it seems to me that sometimes politics and world affairs align in such a way that the year can lead to too much death and destruction on both the domestic and international scenes. Such events cause major changes, both physically and emotionally.

1968 was such a year, bracketing as it did the capture of the U.S.S. Pueblo, the Tet Offensive in Vietnam, the My Lai Massacre, the Washington Riots and other civil disturbances after the murder of Dr. Martin Luther King, Jr., the withdrawal of President Lyndon Johnson from the 1968 campaign, the assassination of Senator Robert F. Kennedy, Resurrection City built on The Mall in Washington, and the brutalization of demonstrators exercising their 1st Amendment Rights at the Chicago Democratic Convention by the Chicago Police Department.

1968 was a difficult year for me personally. The second half was my indoctrination as a 2nd Lieutenant in the U.S. Marine Corps, during which time I was preparing to bet my life on my comrades, and my sister ran away from home in disgust from the treatment of protesters at the Democratic National Convention in Chicago—she never completely returned. Every time I visit Washington, DC, I am reminded of 1968. There are buildings on H Street, NE, within ½ mile of The Capitol Building, which are still boarded up from that time (a shameful reminder and reality about Washington politics).

2012 is stacking up to have similar momentous import. Like the years leading up to 1968, I have been watching as the United States created 100 million new enemies in the Muslim world. I wrote a book about this in 2007, but few read it.

Though I shouted at the gathering darkness, and the long-term impact of America's arrogance in the world during the Bush Administration, we went right on brutalizing the Muslim world.

Things haven't changed much since 1968! The generals and admirals are still resisting downsizing the military, because they know their careers may be stifled; the military-industrial complex, which got us to increase our defense budget by $350 billion per year after 9/11, doesn't want to give up all of their lucrative contracts; and the Neocons are simply trying to pick a fight with Iran, just to keep the defense industry cooking along and sucking all of the juice out of the federal budget, while blaming the budget overruns on Baby Boomers.

I fully expect a major conflagration with Iran within the next few months. Recently the Iranian Navy has been playing cat and mouse with our 5th Fleet, which is a bit of a PR joke. They have about as much hope of successfully fighting the American Navy as a bunch of plastic toy ships in a bathtub with 2-year-old twin boys. But, if they're not careful, someone is going to claim there's been a new Gulf of Tonkin Incident in the Straight of Hormuz (you know, like the one that didn't happen in 1964), and we'll be off to the races once again.

With 2012 being an election year and the incumbent President in some domestic stress, we can expect the Administration to embrace the idea of a conflict with Iran, after building up our tolerance for the idea over the next few months. The whole idea is ludicrous! Based on 2010 numbers, the U.S. spends 98 times as much on Defense as does Iran. Even Saudi Arabia, our ally on the southern side of the Arabian Gulf, spends 6 times as much as Iran on Defense. Israel admits to spending 2 times as much. The Iranian leadership knows these numbers, and knows that pushing Israel and/or the U.S. too far would be the end of their regime. Why would they do that? They're into publicity stunts, but they're not suicidal.

Nonetheless, things can go too far. The idea that Iran would have a nuclear weapon is a boogeyman throughout the region, though the reality of it would be far less dangerous than everyone suggests. While the rhetoric suggests that they would like to wipe out Israel, the reality is far different. First of all, Jerusalem is one of the holiest places in Islam, so Muslims would not want to make it uninhabitable. Secondly, nuclear explosions cause fallout and Iran is down wind from Israel, so any attack on Israel would be an indirect attack of nuclear fallout on Iran itself. And finally, any attack on Israel would bring an immediate and decisive response from the United States resulting in the demise of Iran's theocratic regime.

Unlike the Republican Presidential candidates, who seem to be ready to go to war with Iran at the drop of a hat, at least President Obama has shown a firm hand on the tiller of State. He can be relied upon to take us into a war only if absolutely necessary.

Meanwhile, the demonstrators at home are mad at the powers of Wall Street for destroying our economy, and they are not going to be quiet about it over the coming months. There will be more and more confrontation, probably leading to some ugly incidents. The only way the Republicans will be able to divert attention from the Occupy Movement will be to try to gin up a war with Iran behind the scenes. I'm sorry to be so cynical about our politics, but I've had half a century to observe how things get done.

The good news for Americans is that the United States will survive all of this turmoil. We have enough depth so that no matter how bad things get, nothing much will change for the average American. Of course, we'll all continue to have lighter bank accounts thanks to Wall Street, but the mainstream media won't notice that. I sure wouldn't want to be an Iranian civilian living near Natanz, Isfahan, or any of the other Iranian nuclear facilities.

We watched Seven Days in May the other night. That's the 1964 movie in which Kirk Douglas and Burt Lancaster do battle over a military plot to take over the American government. The issues then were very much the same as the issues today—nothing much has changed! The question for all Americans in 2012 will be the same as then. What kind of a country do we want to have? What kind of a world do we want to have? Are we really a Christian nation that believes in Jesus' teaching of truth, love, and compassion? Or, have the warmongers and arrogant bank cheats that crashed our economy by their greed hijacked Christianity?

One thing I know: I want our Country back!

Personal Morality

Chapter 25: A Personal Morality

"...[T]he investigator comes back to the individual, for what he is all the time concerned with are certain complex thought-forms, the archetypes, which must be conjectured as the unconscious organizers of our ideas. The motive force that produces these configurations cannot be distinguished from the transconscious factor known as instinct. There is, therefore, no justification for visualizing the archetype as anything other than the image of instinct in man." ¶278, Aion, by Dr. Carl G. Jung

All creatures rely on instinct. The favorite proof of that in my household is the Chesapeake Conservancy's Osprey family, Tom, Audrey, and their children, which we watch live every spring and summer as the parents return to the same nesting spot each March, and produce a new family. The most striking feature of this numinous experience is watching Audrey act out the Mother archetype each year. She instinctively knows what to do!

The third week of March every year, she returns to the same platform and waits for Tom to return. When he does, they begin building a nest and mating. Shortly thereafter Audrey produces 3-4 eggs, and then she sits for 40 days after the last one is laid, while the chicks incubate. Tom takes up the sitting duties about 30% of the time, and spends the rest of his time fishing and providing security for Audrey. They never talk about it; they After the babies hatch it's just fish, fish, fish, feed, feed, feed, until the babies, who double in size about every six days, are ready to fly and learn to fish for themselves. Then it's off to Brazil for the winter, where the females flock separately from the males, and then back again the following March to do it all over again. Just like clockwork. Here's the whole

This video can be found on Youtube as " 2013 Year in Review: Tom & Audrey Osprey,"

It doesn't take more to see that these archetypal instincts are common to all in the animal world, including humans. Tom and Audrey are not mammals, and yet you can clearly see the archetype (instinct) of Mother every bit as strongly in Audrey as you see it in any human Mother.

This video can be found on Youtube as " Pete Seeger Kisses Sweeter Than Wine,"

So what sets human beings apart? The answer is civilization. In Audrey's world, Audrey would not hesitate to kill another Osprey, who encroached on her territory. While this rarely happens between birds of a feather, the American Bald Eagles and the Osprey have a constant air war going on all summer long. The Eagles would not hesitate to take one of Audrey's babies home for lunch, and it would not be a social occasion.

In human societies, though, we have learned to tolerate outsiders, to a lesser or stronger degree. In the United States, we have people from every national origin, religion, ethnic group and race. In general, we have learned (against our instinct) to live together in peace, and not molest the peace and security of our neighbors. This is still a problem manifested by racism, but we largely manage to all become that one common instinctive archetype we call American. Other societies have more difficulty, because their groups are much more of the "birds of a feather" variety.

But the instinct of tolerance, learned by every American, is not in the DNA. It must be taught in our schools, and there is always a tension. Today over 40 million Irish Americans live in the United States, while just over 4.5 million live in Ireland. But, in the 1840s, when the Potato Famine hit Ireland, and many emigrated to North America, they were not accepted at first.

The Irish were largely Catholics. The leaders of their religion had tried to force their religion on Protestants for centuries before. People of European descent had settled in North America more than 200 years before, and labeled themselves American as of right. Gradually, they became an homogenous mass of people, who wrested their independence from Europe three generations earlier than the arrival of the Irish.

But the Catholics earned their place beside the Protestants in North America. During the American Revolution, Maryland (founded by Catholics) fought side by side with Massachusetts (founded by Puritan Protestants), and so religion had become less important as a differentiator to most Americans. Still, the flood of Irishmen in the 1840s was a bit of a shock to American civilization. But, by the time the third generation came around, Irishmen had magically become the archetypal policemen of Boston, and that archetype persists to this day.

Each wave of new immigrants has been digested into the great maw of American civilization, and when the archetypal symbol of our flag is hauled out for our defense, we Americans will be shoulder to shoulder, regardless of color, religion, or ethnic heritage.

This is the nature of our civilization. We can learn a new instinct much more quickly than it can be developed by evolution. Ten thousand years from now, Audrey & Tom's descendants will likely be passing the round of life in much the same way, conducting an air war against the Eagles every day, but few would doubt that human civilization will be vastly different.

How do we develop so fast? We do it by each of us, in our own generation, deciding for ourselves what is morally right, and then passing that information on to our children. They in their turn must also decide for themselves, but they will be informed by our experiences and views.

400 years ago I could easily have been burned at the stake for writing even the contents of this essay, because it does challenge some ideas of the Church. And yet, today most Americans would consider this essay perfectly acceptable, regardless of religion.

There are those who believe to this day that one religion is superior to another; one race is superior to another; etc. But The United States of America stands as testament to the lie of those ideas. The rest of the people of the world can rant and rail against the idea all they like, but in the face of our success they cannot claim that they alone have the answers.

Each person, in their own way, must decide for themselves what is good about what we have done in North America and what is genuinely bad. Sometimes our decisions go against instinct. Unlike Tom and Audrey, who only see a predator or an enemy in those other than their own species, we can simply decide for ourselves what is reasonable and moral and what is not.

What will you do to develop your own personal morality? What will you do to pass that sense of morality on to your children? Will you recognize the sources of evil in your own Soul? Will you admit to them and heal them; or will you have your memory be characterized by your bigotry, your abuse of women, and your rigid and regressive attitudes? I remember my maternal grandfather that way, and his attitudes caused me to be his polar opposite politically. How will your children and grandchildren remember you? Will you be remembered as a paragon of the thriving human community, or will you be remembered as an example of a dead world, which is better left buried and forgotten?

Chapter 26: A Personal Disarmament

"Be still, and know that I am God:
I will be exalted among the heathen.
I will be exalted in the earth."
Psalm 46:10, The Holy Bible

Like this 10-week old Osprey, Americans had our feathers ruffled after 9/11, and our acting out in the form of the wars in Iraq and Afghanistan was both a predictable and an unpredictable result. The death and carnage that followed destroyed cultures that had taken millennia to develop, killing hundreds of thousands of innocent people, including nearly 7 thousand Americans. The world will feel the consequences of our reaction for generations.

I will never forget the sly smile that came across President George W. Bush's face, when an aide whispered into his ear that the World Trade Center had been attacked. He had known for at least six weeks that Al Qaeda was planning something big, and he knew that such a pretext would be just what he needed to take the country to war and settle a family grudge against Saddam Hussein. That part of the video of our President sitting in the kindergarten classroom in Florida has now been carefully expunged from the images publicly available, but I am witness to it. I saw the evil shadow that danced across his face.

Since then the Republican Party and many of our fellow Americans have been controlled by fear mongers and hate mongers. They sell fear like soap on our television sets. It is time we took a breath long enough to understand that we cannot shoot every teen in a hoodie; and the world and our country will contain people of every race and religion, no matter what we do; no matter what the consequences.

We have not come to a time when we can beat our swords into plowshares, but we can take a breath and decide the best way forward, for everyone, not the least of whom are our grandchildren.

A 10-week-old Osprey offers us an excellent example. His nature tells him that the appropriate reactions to adversity are either fight or flight. Last summer he found himself in a potentially deadly predicament and did neither. Tens of thousands of people around the world watched in horror as he was inadvertently ensnared in a stray piece of fishing line. Watch what happened next:

This video can be found on Youtube as "Ozzie's Rescue,"

I pray that my countrymen will follow his example.

Note: He did not fly away.
He learned from his experience and disarmed his instincts.

Chapter 27: Answer to Job

"...What most people overlook or seem unable to understand is the fact that I regard the psyche as real. They believe only in physical facts, and must consequently come to the conclusion that either the uranium itself or the laboratory equipment created the atom bomb. That is no less absurd than the assumption that a non-real psyche is responsible for it. God is an obvious psychic and non-physical fact, i.e., a fact that can be established psychically but not physically. ... ¶751

*"...Clearly, the material evidence for the existence of this psychic phenomenon is more than sufficient. It does not matter at all that a physically impossible fact is asserted, because all religious assertions are physical **impossibilities.** If they were not so, they would, as I said earlier, necessarily be treated in the text-books of natural science.* **But religious statements without exception have to do with the reality of the psyche and not with the reality of the physis.**" ¶752, Answer to Job, C.G. Jung

I'm sure it might seem odd that I feel compelled to write a review of Dr. Carl G. Jung's Answer to Job, more than 63 years after it was written, but the questions it answers are palpable in the psyche of human beings right now, and it provides many answers beyond the obvious one:

Why was God so cruel to Job?

The more pressing questions Answer to Job addresses for the 21st Century, among many others, are:

What is wrong with fundamentalism in Christianity?

Why are atheists wrong in writing off God based on the scientific evidence?

Why are the Republicans right in their anxiety about the candidacy of Hillary Clinton for President of the United States in 2016?

How could Dr. Jung answer, when asked if he believed in God, "I don't need to believe. I know"?

What is the greatest danger to the future of humanity today?

****

Why was God so cruel to Job?

Dr. Jung speaks of Job and Yahweh in a psychological sense, rather than a religious sense. He points out that Yahweh did not consult His omniscience when accepting the wager of Satan that Job's faith could be subverted. Rather, He let the whims of His dark side, Satan, run amok. The clergy have broadly condemned this book for pointing out that the God of light and goodness, Whom they have sold humanity for several thousand years, has a dark side within Himself.

If Yahweh had consulted His omniscience, He would have known what the result would be. He would have known that Job would maintain his faith in the Almighty regardless of what calamities befell him and his family. In this way, Job was much like the people of the American Midwest and South, who praise the will of God despite being visited annually by terrible tornadoes and hurricanes.

By his analysis, Dr. Jung posits that Job was more moral than Yahweh in that time, or at least, as a manifestation of Yahweh's morality incarnate, has access to decisions of morality, which come from the consciousness of humanity itself. At the time of Job, Yahweh was still willing to play with Job, as a cat would play with a mouse in a box, rather than take the moral high road and consult His omniscience to know what the result would be from the wager with Satan.

One can infer that here is where Christianity has failed mankind over the past two thousand years. It has allowed men to project their darkness outside of themselves, and onto a being outside of God, Satan, rather than understanding that these forces are within us all. Only if we accept that we have such darkness in our own unconscious do we have any hope of dealing with it consciously and morally.

Failing that conscious understanding is precisely how the scandals emerge, which fill many of our daytime television broadcasts and political newscasts. These again let us project our darkness on those terrible people, who dance before our eyes, and let us believe that if so-in-so can be so immoral, then I myself must not be so bad. But this illusion allows us to kid ourselves.

Dr. Jung is merely swiping away the illusion, that makes so many Christians "feel good," even though each one of us harbors evil and must deal with its moral ambiguity each day. President Jimmy Carter "almost scuttled his first presidential campaign simply by admitting to a magazine journalist that he'd 'committed adultery in his heart ' (without actually doing anything about it!)," because Christians want the illusion that our leaders are moral and without a dark side. Here President Carter essentially assumed the role of Job, by admitting to his own darkness, but like Job, he was rewarded for his moral confession with the Presidency. Who can say that the reward did not come from God, just as Job was rewarded for his faith?

The more pressing questions Answer to Job addresses for the 21st Century, among many others, are:

What is wrong with fundamentalism in Christianity?

Dr. Jung points out that fundamentalism gives no room for the religion to breathe. Though he was the son of a Swiss Reformed Protestant pastor, he extolls The Assumption of the Virgin Mary into Heaven , a Papal Bull of Pope Pius XII published in 1950, which he considered "to be the most important religious event since the Reformation." ¶752, Answer to Job, by C.G. Jung. He particularly liked it, because it

> *"expresses a renewed hope for the fulfillment of that yearning for peace which stirs deep down in the soul, and for a resolution of the threatening tension between the opposites.* Everyone shares this tension and everyone experiences it in his individual form of unrest, the more so the less he sees any possibility of getting rid of it by rational means." ¶754, Answer to Job, C.G. Jung

He observes that Pope Pius's announcement, which has the authority of "Papal infallibility," was based on the willingness of the Catholic Church to give

"*the archetypal symbolisms the necessary freedom and space in which to develop over the centuries while at the same time insisting on their original form, unperturbed by intellectual difficulties and the objections of rationalists. In this way the Catholic Church demonstrates her maternal character, because she allows the tree growing out of her matrix to develop according to its own laws. **Protestantism, in contrast, is committed to the paternal spirit.***" ¶754, Answer to Job, C.G. Jung

Though a lifelong Protestant himself, Dr. Jung pulls no punches when commenting on Protestantism:

"*The logical consistency of the papal declaration cannot be surpassed, and it leaves Protestantism with the odium of being nothing but a man's religion which allows no metaphysical representation of woman. ... Protestantism has obviously not given sufficient attention to the signs of the times which point to the equality of women.*" ¶753

"*It **would be desirable for the Protestant** to understand that the new dogma has placed upon him a new responsibility toward the worldly spirit of our age, for **he cannot simply deny his problematic sister before the eyes of the world.** He must, even if he finds her antipathetic, be fair to her if he does not want to lose his self-respect.... Considering the arbitrary and protean state of his own dogmas ... he cannot afford to remain rigid and impervious to the spirit of the age.* ¶754, Answer to Job, C.G. Jung

Why are atheists wrong in writing off God based on the scientific evidence?

The often heard complaint about religion by atheists is that none of it can be proven in the temporal world. As pointed out in the beginning of this essay, Dr. Jung simply pointed out that

"religious statements without exception have to do with the reality of the psyche and not with the reality of the physis." ¶752, Answer to Job, C.G. Jung

After more than a century of the modern development of psychotherapy and its efficacy, there can be no doubt that the psyche exists, and that it is tremendously powerful in the well being of all human beings. In order to deny this fact, atheists would have to deny that they dream and that their heart beats, and it seems unlikely that many could do that without giving rise to a serious concern about their own mental health.

Dr. Jung's point quite simply is that the content of religions, all of them, are psychic facts, the existence of which cannot be denied. It makes no difference whatever that they do not exist in the temporal world that we can physically touch, because that is not their domain. They are among the primary stuff of the psyche, and in this sense there can be no doubt that God, in all manifestations both male and female and in the pleroma itself, does exist. Moreover, God does exist in precisely the manifestation found in every religion and spiritual tradition found within the human species. **Why are the Republicans right in their anxiety about the candidacy of Hillary Clinton for President of the United States in 2016?**

"What outrages the Protestant standpoint in particular is ... the endangered supremacy of Christ, from which Protestantism will not budge ... it **leaves Protestantism with the odium of being nothing but a man's religion** *which allows no metaphysical representation of woman. ...* **Protestantism has obviously not given sufficient attention to the signs of the times which point to the equality of women. ..."** ¶752-753, Answer to Job, C.G. Jung

What Dr. Jung observed in 1951, in his comments on The Assumption of the Virgin Mary into Heaven in 1950, is that the feminine principle is emerging. After the emergence of the Women's Movement since Susan B. Anthony in the late 19th Century, it would be impossible for anyone who is awake to deny this. She's coming as inexorably as a freight train, and the hope she represents is what a desperately divided world needs right now.

Most significantly,

> *"The new dogma [The Assumption of the Virgin Mary into Heaven in 1950] expresses a renewed hope for the fulfillment of that yearning for peace which stirs deep down in the soul, and for a resolution of the threatening tension between the opposites.* Everyone shares this tension and everyone experiences it in his individual form of unrest, the more so the less he sees any possibility of getting rid of it by rational means." ¶754, Answer to Job, C.G. Jung

**How could Dr. Jung answer, when asked if he believed in God,
"I don't need to believe. I know"?**

This video can be found on Youtube as "Quote: Carl Jung.. I know God exists,"

Dr. Jung was, by most who acknowledge his significance regardless of how controversial his views became, the most prominent psychologist of the Twentieth Century. Originally working with Dr. Sigmund Freud, he served as a midwife to the very concept of psychotherapy itself. As The Red Book has shown the world, since its emergence in 2009, he truly knew the parameters of the human psyche first hand, more than any of his contemporaries. When he made the following statement, he knew what he was talking about from first hand experience:

> *"But religious statements without exception have to do with the reality of the psyche and not with the reality of the physis."* ¶752, Answer to Job, C.G. Jung

What is the greatest danger to the future of humanity today?

"The World hangs on a thin thread, and that is the psyche of man. *Nowadays we are not threatened by elementary catastrophes. There is no such thing as an H-bomb. That is all man's doing. We are the great danger. Psyche is the great danger. What if something goes wrong with the Psyche?*

"And so it is demonstrated to us in our days, what the power of the psyche is of man. How important it is to know something about it. But we know NoThing about it.

"Nobody would give credit to the idea that the psychical processes of the ordinary man have any importance whatever. One thinks, "Oh, he is just what he has in his head. It is all from his surroundings. He is taught such and such a thing, believes such and such a thing, and particularly if he is well-housed and well-fed, then he has no ideas at all. **That's the great mistake,** *because he is just that which he is born, and he is not born as a tabula rasa, but as a reality."*

From the interview, "Face to Face with Carl Jung," available in its entirety on YouTube.

As the paragraph numbers in the quotes above suggest, there is much more to Answer to Job than these few paragraphs have highlighted. Here is the greatest psychologist of the 20th Century, near the end of his long life of prodigious scholarship, making his case to the high court of the ages. It is a masterstroke! As Dr. Jung said himself in a letter to Aniella Jaffé, "I have landed the great whale; I mean 'Answer to Job.'" Sonu Shamdasani's Foreword to the 2010 Edition, P. viii, *Answer to Job*, C.G. Jung.

I found that many of Dr. Jung's observations were quite funny in the context of the late 20th Century and early 21st Century, much of which he predicted in his book. At the very least, it answered many questions I have struggled with in religion for my whole life.

Chapter 28: Do You Believe in God?

"Thus my God found salvation. He was saved precisely by what one would actually consider fatal, namely by declaring him a figment of imagination. How often has it been assumed that the Gods have been brought to their end in this way. This was obviously a serious mistake, since this was precisely what saved the God. He did not pass away, but became a living fantasy, whose workings I could feel on my own body: my inherent heaviness faded and the hot and cold way of pain no longer burned and froze my soles. The weight no longer kept me pressed to the ground, but instead the wind carried me lightly like a feather, while I carried the giant." Dr. Carl G. Jung, *The Red Book (Reader's Edition, Pp. 295-96)*

First, watch this video! This video can be found on Youtube as "The Hubble Ultra Deep Field in 3D"

Did you see God in that video? Some of you might have, I suppose. Today we can look back to within 500,000 years of the Big Bang, almost to where the first light ever escaped from anything—13.7 billion years. Last summer human beings finally observed (I can't say "saw") the Higgs Boson, the smallest thing ever actually found, by using an instrument that is 17 miles in circumference, and cost billions of dollars. Some have even called the Higgs Boson "The God Particle" (although many Physicists call it the "God Damned Particle"), although that was more public relations than anything truly relating to all or part of a supreme being. So where is God?

Dr. Carl G. Jung, the most famous psychologist of the 20th Century, said quite a few startling things. Some of them went as follows:

1) Dr. Jung was the son of a country pastor, who had lost his faith. When asked whether he believed in God on the BBC, he famously answered, **"I don't need to believe, I know."**

2) When talking about the psyche, after a career of writing about it so extensively that his collected works fill a large bookshelf, he said, "How important is it to do something about it? **But we know NOthing about it."** The emphasis came through in English because of his German accent, but we get the point.

3) When talking about fantasy, dreams and visions he said, **"These are facts. These are psychic facts."** Surely none of us can deny this perspective. When you have a dream or nightmare, it is quite real to you. Dr. Jung also pointed out that absolutely nothing has been created by man, or any other creature we know of for that matter, without it first having been a fantasy in the mind of the creator.

His point in *The Red Book* quote is that each and every one of us has a different image of what God is. Even atheists cannot deny the driving force in their unconscious, which causes them to do various things. A psychologist, speaking as a scientist or person of medicine, might call these unconscious energies, or intuitions, or synchronicities. Heck, even Nobel Prize Laureate Wolfgang Pauli spent 26 years corresponding with Dr. Jung about such matters as if they are quite real.

But the point is that the "sky God" of the Sistine Chapel and of Greek Mythology, is psychologically a projection of what is within the Souls of humanity. As astronomers have found, there is no such thing that science can point to with assurance. Except in the sense that Dr. Jung has spoken of it in the quote above. A God is a part of all of us, but for each of us it is different.

"No, no, no," you say! "I am a Christian or a Muslim or a Jew or a Hindu or a Jain or a Buddhist, and my God is [this way] or [that way]."
Is it really?
If I select any word at random, let's say, "Boat," each one of us will envision it in a somewhat different way. Is it the Queen Mary or the Kontiki or a rowboat or a gravy boat or a rowboat or a yacht, and if it is a "yacht" is it a larger power cruiser like an Arab prince might own or a sailing yacht, and if so how big. "Yacht" is one of 12 Dutch words in the English language, and its literal translation is "small boat," so what does that mean? You see what I'm getting at, I think.

So it is with the "God" of our religions. If we are Christians or Muslims, our ideas might generally track, partially because we have used the ultimate method of selecting our congregation, beheading and warfare, as a means of weeding out anyone that didn't think pretty much just like us. But the truth is that if you ask a fellow follower of any religion, pick one it doesn't matter, you will be surprised to find that, when you say "God," the word pretty much means something different to every human being you might meet, regardless of religion. In point of fact, all words work exactly that way, as I've illustrated above. So let's get over the beheading stuff, and start to see each of our fellow human beings as just like us in the sense that each one of us is completely different. That would be a refreshing perspective for a change, don't you think?

As for the question of, "Do you believe in God?", I'm with Dr. Jung, I don't have to believe, I know. How about you?

Chapter 29: God Has Spoken!

"The idea of God is an absolutely necessary psychological function of an irrational nature, which has nothing whatever to do with the question of God's existence."
Dr. Carl G. Jung

I am not the Messiah! But I do know when God speaks and when not. God works wonders in many mysterious ways.

Last week a venal fundamentalist preacher claimed that Hurricane Sandy was God's punishment of the people of New York and New Jersey for allowing Gay marriage, failing to notice that New Jersey has not yet legalized Gay marriage. He set himself up for my claim that Hurricane Sandy was God's way of showing undecided voters that President Barack Obama should win Election 2012.

If we take my characterization a step further, Election 2012 then defined God's intention on several key questions that have bedeviled the American electorate for generations. These are:

1. Women are God's children just as much as men, and God did not intend for one to hold dominion over the other. God intended for the feminine and masculine principles to be equal partners in the development of our species.

2. God shows us that all human beings should have the privilege of Love, which is infinite. Love is not restricted to one thing or another. I Love my wife, yes, but I also still Love the Black Marine who died in my arms on a mountainside in Vietnam, defending the Country we both Love. My Love for him is not defined by the color of his skin, nor by his gender, but by our shared devotion to the principles that make the United States strong. I believe that those principles are built on the foundation of Love itself. Americans, who have thought

about it compassionately, know that God has not limited Love in any way, and it is wrong for human beings to constrain what God has made infinite. Maryland, Maine, Minnesota and Washignton have approved the concept of same-sex marriage, and it is inevitable that the rest of the Country will follow suit.

3. God has shown us that all human beings should be respected for their contribution to society. In Maryland, God has caused us to vote in favor of the Dream Act, which allows immigrants who contribute to the community to enjoy many of the benefits of citizenship. After all, if we look at history, every person in North and South America, and I include within this the so-called "native Americans," is descended from people who came from somewhere else, or they came from somewhere else themselves.

4. God has shown us again the same thing that God has shown clearly since our species began walking on the Earth: Compassion trumps greed every time.

5. God has shown us in the elections of Elizabeth Warren (MA), Tammy Duckworth (IL), Claire McCaskill (MO), Maizie Hirono (HI), Tammy Baldwin (WI), Diane Feinstein (CA), Deborah Fischer (NE), Amy Klobuchar (MN), Maria Cantwell (WA), and Debbie Stabenow (MI) that women can and do make outstanding legislators and can represent Liberty as well
as men.

6. God has shown us by the defeat of Richard Mourdock by Joe Donnelly and Todd Akin by Claire McCaskill that rape and its consequences are not gifts.

7. God has shown us by the elections in California, Colorado, and Washington that it is time to rethink the war on drugs, which has filled our prisons without benefitting society.

8. God has clearly told the "fundamentalist" Christians that it is time to reevaluate their interpretation of Christ's message of Truth, Love and Compassion.

9. And God has emphatically told Republicans that they DO have to cater to women, to Latinos, and to the LGBT community. Chris Christie take note!

Chapter 30: The Glory of God

"The marked tendency of the western democracies to internal dissension is the very thing that could lead them into a more hopeful path." Dr. Carl G. Jung, CW10, P. 225

As we face the next two weeks of political conventions and the following two months of quarrelsome electioneering, the rest of the world must think that Americans are crazy. But there is method in our madness. In honor of my fellow Americans, many of whom will put their emotions on the line in the next two months, I decided to republish this somewhat revised version of Chapter 6 of my 2007 book, *Tsunami of Blood:*

"What one factor, above all others, makes the United States of America the strongest country in the World?" When I ask my question the response is often angst. Few have actually thought about what makes America strong. I get responses from Ph.D.s, which can only be regarded as stammering. So, why do I ask it? I ask it to point out that dissension is part and parcel of the American experience.

The strength of America comes from its Diversity. We have so many national, religious and ethnic groups, in North America, that our country has experienced a process of tempering, like making steel. Impurities of the human condition are forced out over time.

Put in terms of ideas, whenever a good idea surfaces, from whatever ethnic group, all of the other groups accept it immediately. Since it is global, my favorite example is Starbuck's. I have often worked in a hospital in Riyadh, Saudi Arabia, where there are four Starbuck's coffee shops within the building. This proves that when an idea is good, not only do all Americans adopt it, but everyone adopts it.

When a bad idea is launched from one group, however, all of the other groups pound it out of the system. This is, at best, a messy and noisy process, and at worst can be a very bloody process. My example for a bad idea is slavery. For nearly 250 years, slavery was practiced in North America. Finally, we fought our Civil War over the issue, killing tens of thousands of men and women. In 1863, slavery was abolished by Abraham Lincoln in the Emancipation Proclamation. We still suffer in this strongest country in the World from the fallout of that bad idea. We have racial hatreds, and poor black minorities still. But the messy and noisy change is on, and things have improved dramatically in my lifetime.

In 1957, the Governor of Virginia closed all of the schools in the State to avoid integrating. I experienced that because I missed a semester of my 7th grade year, until my parents were able to move my family to Pennsylvania. Today, that ugly episode of American history seems far behind us, and, in the last decade, I have only met one person, to whom I mentioned it, who even knew it ever happened. But it did; and it happened to Americans!

So yes, it is absolutely true that the United States is not perfect. It is now, and ever will be, a work in progress. Our Founding Fathers could not possibly have imagined what it would become when they put their signatures to the Declaration of Independence, risking execution for treason, and proclaimed "that all men are created equal. They are endowed by their creator with certain inalienable rights. That among these are life, liberty and the pursuit of happiness." Many of them were slave owners, but they knew the system would somehow have to change, much as many of today's world leaders live knowing that their systems are unjust, and that women and men of conviction and courage will change them violently (as we Americans have done), if they are not changed by their leaders in a responsible and ethical manner. This is inevitable. Our Founding Fathers put their names, their lives, and their fortunes on the line for principles, the long-term effect of which even they could not have imagined. But, the 236-year tempering process, of good ideas adopted and bad ideas hammered out of the system, which really started with the first colonists, in 1607, has created the strongest (if not the greatest) country on the planet. Over the past decade, I have mused on my idea that diversity is the reason for the strength of the United States many times. It occurred to me that when I meet an American in my business life, or any other nationality for that matter, of a different race, ethnic or religious background, I rejoice, because I know that they will bring a new perspective to the business problems we face together, and make our company stronger. I know that many of my countrymen have not consciously thought about the strength of the United States in this way, and would not agree, but perhaps it will become a mantra across our land, and make us better for it.

On one occasion, much later in my story, I referred to *diversity* as The Glory of God. It occurred to me that God made us all, regardless of skin tone or religion we follow. Indeed, God created all religions, did S/he not? I have raised this point many times, and most have agreed on this point. And so I will assert that it is true for the whole World we live in, that *Diversity is the Glory of God*, and when everyone in the World accepts and believes that truth, all of our children will live in peace everywhere.

Chapter 31: First Burn All of the Bibles

My Christian fundamentalist friends and family will call the title of this piece a sacrilege. Therein lies the fundamental problem of our time; because my Muslim friends would feel the same if I used the name of the Qu'ran (Koran) in the title of this piece. Before we all destroy ourselves over the literal meaning of one book or another, and their ultimate Truth, let's stop and reflect.

This essay is about how we have all missed God's point. Dr. Carl G. Jung elucidated the problem in *The Red Book:*

> *"You must know one thing above all: a succession of words does not have only one meaning. But men strive to assign only a single meaning to the sequence of words, in order to have an unambiguous language. This striving is worldly and constricted, and belongs to the deepest layers of the divine creative plan. On the higher levels of insight into divine thoughts, you recognize that the sequence of words has more than one valid meaning. Only to the all-knowing is it given to know all the meanings of a sequence of words. Increasingly we try to grasp a few more meanings."* [The Red Book by C.G. Jung, P. 267; Reader's Edition P. 244]

The point is that the Divine Mystery is far beyond our poor power to add or detract. Metaphorically, if we think of the light of the universe in the darkness of space, we see how super human the task is to mere mortals, even divinely inspired ones. Physicists tell us that light has properties of both waves and particles, and that it travels at a given speed. But if it has those properties, why do those waves and particles not collide and interfere with one another infinitely in the darkness of space?

But light reaches us from infinite sources and reflects off our bodies and minds. We can describe it and reflect it, but we cannot fully explain it. Why? It's a mystery. E=mc2 Such a simple equation symbolizes a lifetime of work, a much longer equation, has not yet been superseded, and yet it is neither the truth behind what it represents, nor is it perfect. Physicists still cannot explain 90% of the universe, though they know it is there.

The Bible does talk about the fact that we can be witnesses to light, but it clearly suggests that we are not the Light. In the same sense as a planet can reflect the mystery of light, so a human being or a word can reflect some aspect of totality. Think of the light in space metaphor in reading this passage from John I:1-10:

> "And the light shineth in darkness, and the darkness comprehended it not. There was a man sent from God, whose name was John. The same came for a witness, to bear witness of the Light, that all men through him might believe. He was not that Light, but was sent to bear witness of that Light. That was the true Light, which lighteth every man that cometh into the world. He was in the world, and the world was made by him, and the world knew him not.

There is a terrible consequence of our ignorance of putting all of our faith in one interpretation of the divine mystery or another person's vision. Dr. Jung describes the consequence in explaining the phenomenon of World War I:

> "But what happened to my day? Torches were kindled, bloody anger and disputes erupted. As darkness seized the world, the terrible war arose and the darkness destroyed the light of the world, since it was incomprehensible to the darkness and good for nothing anymore. And so we had to taste Hell.

> "I saw which vices the virtues of this time changed into, how your mildness became hard, your goodness became brutality, your love became hate, and your understanding became madness. Why did you want to comprehend the darkness! But you had to or else it would have seized you. Happy the man who anticipates this grasp.

"Did you ever think of the evil in you? Oh, you spoke of it, you mentioned it, and you confessed it smilingly, as a generally human vice, or a recurring misunderstanding. But did you know what evil is, and that it stands precisely right behind your virtues, that it is also your virtues themselves, as their inevitable substance? You locked Satan in the abyss for a millennium, and when the millennium had passed, you laughed at him, since he had become a children's fairy tale. But if the dreadful great one raises his head, the world winces. The most extreme coldness draws near." [The Red Book by C.G. Jung, P. 274; Reader's Edition P. 265]

Is this the Spirit of our Age? Surely we have seen the visage of "the dreadful great one" in all his horrific reality. We have seen him in battles between Christian and Muslim, between Christian and Jew, between Jew and Muslim, between Hindu and Muslim, between Hispanic and White, between Black and White, between Japanese and Chinese ad infinitum. But we know that carrying the battle to its logical conclusion would quite simply rain Hell upon the Earth once again.

Are we mere flotsam on the winds of time, witnesses to a false light, buffeted by the intractable dreadful great one? Or do we, can we, reflect the future of our species in the Light?

Chapter 32: The Apocalypse Is Spread Upon the Earth and Men Do Not See it

The Mayans were right, if they ever did predict the end of the world. But it is the end of the world as we know it, not yet the end of our planet and all life. That time will come, but we now know that Earth will likely be here for four billion or so more years, and life will likely still be here for much of that time, though the future of humanity itself might not be so long.

Jesus Christ came along at an apocalyptic time, when the old Greek and Roman gods were yielding to new ideas about something central. In the early Twenti-eth Century, Carl Jung defined that something psychologically as the Self—"the central archetype of order and meaning that is constellated in the collective unconscious." But to the less knowledgeable humans of fifteen hundred to twenty-five hundred years ago, this central archetype was called The One (by Buddha), God the Father (by Christ and his predecessor Rabbis), and Allah (by The Prophet {PBUH}). Other religious traditions used other names, of course.

But the problem we have today is a new Truth is being revealed and The Apocalypse is upon us. All of us have that secret sinking feeling deep within us that whatever religious tradition we have followed is not the whole story. Yes, fundamentalist Christians and Muslims rave at their less strident fellows and one another, swearing that they have the one true way, but there are few among them who lack this secret doubt.

How can one believe in an outward "sky god" when we can see back to the Big Bang, thanks to the Hubble telescope, and we can see down to infinitesimally small particles thanks to the Large Hadron Collider? Yes, recently the scientists at CERN near Geneva have found a new particle, but in all of their research there is no sign of an external God, per se. Where is Heaven? Where is Hell? Our religious leaders, who insist on the ideas of our ancient forebears, simply look more and more out of touch from the Universe in which we actually live.

This Truth is a terrific shock to the system—globally! It is said that Christianity took 600 years to coalesce into an identifiable religion; the Bible as we know it was not even settled upon until 325 A.D. (at the 1st Council of Nicaea); and Islam was not settled until hundreds of years after the time of The Prophet (PBUH). But the breakup and coalescence of new human ideas about who we are and what we need to do to assure the continuation of our species cannot wait that long.

Professor Carl Jung identified the collective unconscious, and showed that it was common to all human beings, regardless of race, station in life, or creed. What he meant was that society as a whole (globally) is, in effect, a collective organism, with a tendency to manifest its Self (or God) in a way unique from all other creatures. In times of lesser information and communication, this Self manifested in different ways of looking at its mystery, that is, in various religions and concepts of God. But today, those old ideas cannot stand up to the Truths that reveal themselves second by second in our global communication and connection via the Internet and social networks.

In my 2007 book, Tsunami of Blood, I worried that foreign Muslim fundamentalist fighters in Iraq would return to their countries and instigate a global rising up of the burgeoning younger generation of the Muslim world against the West. But, I underestimated by quite a margin the impact of Internet based social networks on younger Muslims. As we saw in the Arab Spring, most young Muslims want the same Human Rights that Americans want. It remains to be seen whether I was truly prescient by predicting the "Islamic State".

Young Muslim women, who find themselves constrained in their home environments, don't hesitate to exercise the rights of Western women when they travel abroad. Of course, they comply with the traditions of Islam, but even those constraints may be breaking down. At the same time, even Bible thumping Christians, who will tell you that every word of the Bible is absolutely true, are being forced to acknowledge that passages like Leviticus 20:13 and 1 Timothy 6:1 are no longer appropriate in the modern world.

As Professor Jung pointed out in his Archetype of the Apocalypse, there has been a revelation and judgment that the old ideas are no longer true, and they are in the process of being destroyed—broken asunder. As human beings, we do not yet know how the new Truth will emerge. The Internet may allow it to emerge quickly, in only a few decades, but it will surely be quite different.

The old ideas of nation states will surely break down. The Royal Society recently published a population study of what will happen between now and 2050. By the middle of this century humanity will have added another 2.3 billion people to our planet, at the current rate. That is equivalent to adding another India and another China within the next 38 years! To support that, we have to add a city of 1 million people every 5 days for the next 38 years! Long before then, India will run out of fresh water sufficient to support its population. If we, in America, think that catastrophe among many will be far away from us and we need not worry about it, we are sadly mistaken. Just the consequences of that one dislocation will be vast and varied across the entire globe.

As a species, we are going to need to wake up from our long slumber of complacency, because the Apocalypse is upon us, and it will not be over until we have either agreed on new models of society for the future of our species or we have destroyed ourselves, and left the planet to our ancient ancestors, the microbes. These issues are not in the remote future, as some may believe and will argue. These issues are for us to resolve. If we leave the work for our children and our grandchildren, the Apocalypse may be far more than just a Jungian archetype talked about in intellectual circles.

The Royal Society's study, which no one can reasonably deny, establishes the urgency of this mission of developing the new Truth for our species. If religions don't modernize, they will become irrelevant. Adolph Hitler and Hideki Tojo proved that you can make good people believe something very wrong for a long period of time, but eventually good people speak up and say, "The Emperor wears no clothes!"

Chapter 33: The Hidden Shame of Republican Policies

"Coal mine, moonshine, or movin' on down the line." Dialogue from *"Coal Miner's Daughter" (1980)*

The political neglect that a poverty map of the United States represents was depicted in the 1980 movie "Coal Miner's Daughter," which showed the truth of the poor side of American life.

This video can be found on Youtube as "Coal miner's daughter (1980) full length trailer"

The talking heads of Fox NewsTM can rant and rave all they like, but there are a few Red State/Blue State facts that simply cannot be denied. Many of the states of the United States, which have followed Republican policies for generations, are the poorest in the United States. It is plain to see from a poverty map a summary of what happens as a result of Republican policies since the Civil War. Many of my Republican friends will tell me those used to be Democrat states, and I will be the first to agree. But what happened since the Civil War is that the two parties have basically swapped policies. This is a classic example of the concept Dr. Carl G. Jung called "enantiodromia," the tendency of things to turn into their opposite.

Like the famous Country/Western singing star Loretta Lynn, smart women left places like that long ago. The result has been a shallowing of the gene pool. From personal experience, I can vouch for the fact that in some of these areas, the people who remained are clearly physically disadvantaged as compared to other Americans.

Fundamentalist Christians, who don't believe in evolution, predominate in many of these areas. It is no wonder, because if the people were bright enough to understand what Republican policies have done to their communities, they would have voted Democrat long ago. If they saw what I have seen, they would have understood that they have tended to push the smart boys and girls away.

In one area I have visited over 200 times, since 1986, the only choices for work are coal mines or retail establishments with predominantly minimum wage jobs. Yes, they do have a shopping mall, but when you look at the people in that mall they clearly seem duller and more beaten down than any other Americans I know. Many people with common sense left areas like that as soon as they understood the limitations of their opportunities, leaving behind the highest percentages of high school dropouts in the country.

It is clear that these are the people, who are willing to vote against their own economic self-interest for reasons that make no real difference to their lives. No babies will be saved if abortion is illegal. No one is inconvenienced by the sexual behaviors of gay lovers. Universal health insurance saves money, because it stops poor people from going to expensive emergency rooms when they need healthcare. Destroying the American public education system has only kept them from seeing what is really happening to them. Since only low wage jobs persist in those regions, they are only too happy to buy cheap Chinese products at WalmartTM, despite the fact that those Chinese manufacturing jobs used to be in the United States.

This is just a sad state of affairs. Follow the link in the map credit below, to see four other maps, which show similar results, proving that the results of Republican policies are simply shameful.

Chapter 34: My Grandfather's Fiancé Didn't Have a Flu Shot and My Grandmothers Had Abortions

Every year when flu season comes around, I urge all of my friends to get a flu shot. Ironically, I wouldn't be here if my Grandfather's fiancé had gotten one. You see, at the time of the great flu epidemic of 1918, my Grandfather was about to marry someone who was not my Grandmother.

Fortunately for me, she and her four sisters died on the same weekend from the Influenza Pandemic of 1918. A pandemic is an epidemic that infects a large proportion of the world's population on a global scale. Statistics vary, but reports put the number of deaths globally that year at 50-100 million. Even now the number of flu related deaths ranges from 3,000 to 49,000 per year, according to the Centers for Disease Control and Prevention.

As a result of the 1918 outbreak, I can honestly say that my daughters, grandchildren, and I would not be here without influenza. We cannot even imagine the tragedy felt by that one family, and my Grandfather, when they lost so many dear ones suddenly. But life goes on, and my Grandfather married my Grandmother. Making the decision about getting a flu shot may amount to making a decision about this kind of parallel universe.

Abortions amount to an even more difficult life or death decision, as they relate to the future of both the parents and the child. I am against abortion, personally. But, I favor the decision to have an abortion to be the decision of the mother rather than society at large. We had a society like that before Roe v. Wade, and it was shameful in many respects.

In the two weeks before my Mother died, she revealed to me a long held deep dark secret. Both of my Grandmothers had abortions. One had two and the other three. I don't know which was which. Those abortions must have taken place in the 1920s, when the choices were coat hangers, abortionists in dark allies, or a few brave doctors, who risked felony convictions for assisting. Many women died in the process.

We cannot know how the world would have been different if these five aunts and uncles would have been born, but I do know that my family is the result of our random luck.

I do understand why the abortion "debate" is such an effective smoke screen for the Republican Party to hide the fact that they are giving away our birthright as Americans to Wall Street bankers, who want to gamble like drunken sailors and grind down the middle class with impunity. Abortion is a difficult and painful topic for nearly everyone, regardless of which side of the political spectrum you vote. But, what I can say to those who don't remember the time before 1973, and who have had the luxury of effective birth control methods all of their lives, is that making abortion illegal will be much worse for society.

The truth is that banning abortion will save exactly zero babies. Any woman who is motivated to make the tragic decision to abort a pregnancy can easily get one outside the United States. All we would do by prohibiting abortion once again would be to brutalize our society. There is nothing gained by sending women who cannot afford an international trip back to their well-meaning sorority sisters, abortion pill smugglers, and backyard butchers.

From my point of view, every time I hear the topic come up, I immediately recognize it as part of the smoke and mirrors that has let the Masters of the Universe create our corrupt and unfair economic system.

A decision about whether to have the influenza vaccine injected into our body is a personal one, but this article points out that it can be a life or death decision to avert or lead to tragedy. An abortion is always tragic for someone, and it is surely a life or death decision, but that decision is best made privately.

My mother's revelation was a testament to the courage of women who have to make that decision. From my point of view, my Grandmothers were both conservative American women, who built a Norman Rockwell style life for us. I never would have imagined that at five times in their youth they were faced with such horrifying and tragic decisions—to break the law and end their pregnancies. I am just glad they allowed my Mother and Father to come to full term.

Who knows what parallel universes would have existed if there was influenza vaccine in 1918 and/or if my Grandmothers had access to proper birth control? I surely can make no judgments at this point of time. But I can say that both of these questions we now face lead to life and death decisions, which need to be made seriously, without putting the fabric of our society at risk.

Chapter 35: A Roadmap for a New Millenium

In Healing the Sacred Divide: Making Peace with Ourselves, Each Other, and the World, Dr. Jean Raffa has provided us with a roadmap for human development for the next millennium. Her crystal clear language has distilled a century of psychological thought into a highly readable primer for the average man or woman. Her book is both an indictment of modern religion, as it is practiced by many, and a pointer toward its promise for the future.

What does it take to find solace, satisfaction, and enlightenment in religion? Fundamentalist religions have used wars and mayhem to widen the gaping hole in our collective psyche. Only by understanding their original calling to wholeness will we fully appreciate their real value to modern society. Dr. Raffa has set a challenge for modern religions of every stripe to "create a new paradigm for humanity" from the Sacred Marriage.

We are raised on pairs of opposites. If we are one thing, we reject the other, but Dr. Raffa points out to us that having loving relationships with otherness is one of three measures of spiritual maturity. She teaches that whatever the Great Mystery of God may be, it also lies within us, and we must find "new ways to imagine and experience God that are consistent with our evolving consciousness." Failure to do so will ultimately mean that modern religions will "wither away under the weight of their own irrelevancy."

Dr. Raffa has infused her insights with compelling stories of her own experiences with the divine. These are embellished by beautiful descriptions of her dreams and other inner work, each of which elucidates another compelling point of her story. Each major section ends with valuable suggestions on how the individual can navigate their own inner journey of spiritual discovery. She has enlivened her work with light and carefree imagined interactions and conversations between God and Goddess, which are fresh, sometimes amusing, and always profound in their import.

In a society of people who have read *Healing the Sacred Divide*, we will have fewer divorces, less crime and mayhem, and a better capacity for living in our shrinking world.

Healing the Sacred Divide: Making Peace with Ourselves, Each Other, and the World received the 2013 Wilbur Award given by the Religion Communicators Council for excellence in communicating religious faith and values in the public arena and for encouraging understanding among faith groups on a national level.

Dr. Jean Raffa is an author, speaker, and leader of workshops, dream groups, and study groups. She maintains a blog called "Matrignosis: A Blog About Inner Wisdom." Her job history includes teacher, television producer, college professor, and instructor at the Disney Institute in Orlando and The Jung Center in Winter Park, FL. She is the author of three books, a workbook, a chapter in a college text, numerous articles in professional journals, and a series of meditations and short stories for Augsburg Fortress Publisher.

Her book The Bridge to Wholeness: A Feminine Alternative to the Hero Myth (Lura-Media, 1992) was nominated for the Benjamin Franklin Award for best psychology book of 1992. Reviewed in several journals and featured on the reading lists of university courses, it was also picked by the Isabella catalogue as a must-read for seeking women.

Dream Theatres of the Soul: Empowering the Feminine Through Jungian Dream-work (Innisfree Press, Inc., 1994) has been used in dreamwork courses throughout the country and is included in Amazon.com's list of the Top 100 Best Selling Dream Books, and TCM's book list of Human Resources for Organizational Development.

The Tea Party – The Good Old Days, Which Never Were

Chapter 36: Is the Tea Party a Psychic Epidemic? Are You a Carrier?

"We are never sure that a new idea will not seize either upon ourselves or upon our neighbors. ... "Homo homini lupus" [the Wolf Man] is a sad yet eternal truism. There is indeed reason enough why man should be afraid of those nonpersonal forces dwelling in the unconscious mind. We are blissfully unconscious of those forces because they never, or almost never, appear in our personal dealings and under ordinary circumstances. But if, on the other hand, people crowd together and form a mob, then the dynamics of the collective man are set free—beasts or demons which lie dormant in every person till he is part of a mob. Man in the crowd is unconsciously lowered to an inferior moral and intellectual level, to that level which is always there, below the threshold of consciousness, ready to break forth as soon as it is stimulated through the formation of a crowd.

"It is, to my mind, a fatal mistake to consider the human psyche as a merely personal affair and to explain it exclusively from a personal point of view. Such a mode of explanation is only applicable to the individual in his ordinary everyday occupations and relationships. If, however, some slight trouble occurs, perhaps in the form of an unforeseen and somewhat extraordinary event, instantly instinctive forces are called up, forces which appear to be wholly unexpected, new and even strange. They can no longer be explained by personal motives, being comparable rather to certain primitive occurrences like panics at solar eclipses and such things. ...

"The change of character that is brought about by the uprush of collective forces is amazing. A gentle and reasonable being can be transformed into a maniac or a savage beast. One is always inclined to lay the blame on external circumstances, but nothing could explode in us if it had not been there. As a matter of fact, we are always living upon a volcano and there is, as far as

we know, no human means of protection against a possible outburst which will destroy everything within its reach. It is certainly a good thing to preach reason and common sense, but what if your audience is a lunatic asylum or a crowd in a collective seizure? *There is not much difference either, because the madman as well as the mob is moved by nonpersonal, overwhelming forces....*

"*....* I always advise my patients to take such obvious but invincible nonsense as the manifestation of a power and a meaning not yet understood. Experience has taught me that it is a much more effective method of procedure to take such a fact seriously and to seek for a suitable explanation. *But an explanation is suitable only when it produces a hypothesis equal to the morbid effect....* It is much better if he understands that his complex *is an autonomous power directed against his conscious personality.* Moreover, such an explanation fits the actual facts much better than a reduction to personal motives. *An apparent personal motivation does exist, but it is not made by intention, it just happens to the patient....*

"*... This is more or less a complete trance, often accompanied by devastating social effects. Even an ordinary emotion can cause a considerable loss of consciousness.* Primitives therefore cherish elaborate forms of politeness [**political correctness?**], speaking with a hushed voice, laying down their weapons, crouching, bowing the head, showing the palms. Even our own forms of politeness still show a "religious" observation of possible psychical dangers. *We propitiate the fates by wishing magically a good day.*"

Dr. Carl G. Jung, Psychology & Religion, The Tavistock Lectures (1937), Pp. 15-19

No one can deny that Americans have faced unforeseen and extraordinary events over the past two decades. Who would have predicted in 1989 that our President would move the entire combat power of the United States Marine Corps and much of the United States Army to Saudi Arabia by 1991, in order to invade Kuwait and Iraq? Who predicted 9/11? Who predicted the financial crash of 2008? Who predicted the election of a black President?

All of these events knocked Americans off their pins, and gave rise to instinctual forces, which no one could have foreseen or controlled. The most obvious of these from a Jungian point of view was 9/11. Within a day American flags flew off the shelves of American stores. The Warrior Archetype was constellated in the American psyche. We were under attack, and we needed to defend ourselves, much as we did after Pearl Harbor. To the barricades!

But who was the enemy? Do we really know to this day? Oh yes, our leaders and venal television commentators have focused our anger and our hate, but who was really at fault? Why were we attacked? Why did our financial system crash, taking our life's savings with it? Was it really because a single mother of two living in Memphis missed a couple of mortgage payments, or even a few thousand such debtors? How could America elect a black man to be our leader?

Yes, Americans had reason enough to react to these major events. But what hath God wrought? The small town America atmosphere of our memory of the late 1970s and 1980s, not to mention the post-WWII era, has been completely erased by a divisive society comparable to nothing we've seen since The Civil War. Indeed, calls for secession from the Union are every bit as common today as they were at that time, and carried on more lips.

But no one can doubt that The Civil War itself was a psychic epidemic in its own right. From the point of view of people in the South, their entire lifestyle was under attack. It was only natural for the Warrior Archetype to be constellated at that time. It has taken over 150 years to calm down those emotions. Many southern states still include the flag of the Confederate States of America in their state flags. What is the subliminal symbolic message there?

When I was a boy living in Norfolk, Virginia in the late 1950s, at the height of the discontent over *Brown v. Board of Education*, which was the U.S. Supreme Court decision that integrated our schools, *The Virginian Pilot* newspaper used to carry little coupons on many pages every single day. They said, "Save your Confederate money, the South will rise again." In my environment of a Navy family from the North, we took this as a kind of joke. But, for the people who paid for those coupons to be published, the battle of The Civil War was still raging, and rages today in the psyches of many of our Southern countrymen! Those instigators were busy trying to undermine the government then. Among other things, Virginia politicians engineered The Stanley Plan, which effectively closed all of the public schools in the state for one year. Even after the United States Supreme Court ruled The Stanley Plan unconstitutional, Governor James Lindsay Almond, Jr. proposed "passive resistance" to integration, which the United States Supreme Court had to rule unconstitutional in 1964 and again in 1968. One can reasonably ask whether this strategy began the movement to magnet schools. The same tactics seem to be the specialty of the Tea Party opposition to the Affordable Care Act today.

The tools of psychic epidemics are plain to see, but that will be the topic of another essay. Here I will just point out that they are the smoke and mirrors of Americas proverbial social issues, used to distract us from the fact that the 1% has used them to distract Americans from their rip off of the American Dream. Their tactics have been relatively open for decades. On August 23, 1971, Lewis F. Powell, Jr. wrote the so-called "Powell Memo" to the Chairman of the Education Committee of the U.S. Chamber of Commerce. It provided the skeleton of the game plan that was played out through the Reagan years and ever since. Every year the American Dream has been slowly pecked away, until it is barely a ghost of its former self.

One induces hypnotic trances by distracting people with many tiny details until they can no longer concentrate on what is really happening. Magicians use a simplified form of this to hide the secrets of their tricks. But, by a constant harangue and distraction on "the social issues," the powers that be have taken us to war, crashed the economy several times with impunity, including most recently requiring a nearly $2 trillion bailout subsequent to the crash that began in earnest in September 2008, and driven millions of Americans out of the workforce. Having ripped off the life's savings of tens of millions of American families, while lining their own pockets massively, they continue to "get away with it" because of the trance they induced among the members of the Tea Party, and, sadly, many loyal Republicans.

Dr. Carl Jung has pointed out to us that far more people have been killed by psychic epidemics than all of the epidemics of disease in human history. The American Civil War, The Spanish American War, The Russian Revolution, World Wars I and II, The Korean War, The Vietnam War, and the various psychic epidemics foisted on their followers by people like Jim Jones at Jonestown, Guyana, David Koresh at Waco. In 2013, Recep Tayyip Erdoğan turned his "Justice and Development Party" (AKP) followers against secular Turks with an effective psychic epidemic, thereby squelching dissent, rather than defending the rights of all Turks, which was his sworn duty.

Osama bin Laden was surely attempting to constellate a psychic epidemic when he planned and executed the 9/11 attacks. He was a terrorist! And in the early days after 9/11, he succeeded. Many in the Muslim world channeled against the United States their frustrations with their lives lived in conditions of tyrannical control. But the hatred he constellated has changed now.

The Muslim Brotherhood's brand of rule has been identified in Egypt and other major Muslim countries, and is on the wane. Their tactics of controlling the vote in several countries have been shown for what they are. The people had to say, "This is Democracy?" Even in Syria, where Al Qaeda was first welcomed by the insurrection against President Bashar Al-Assad, revolutionary Syrians have now turned against bin Laden's descendants, because they now know that they don't want to exchange one tyrant for another.

Who carries a psychic epidemic? As Dr. Jung pointed out, psychic epidemics are really the worst and most dangerous kind. Consider "Typhoid Mary," Mary Mallon, who carried the Typhoid virus in her gall bladder, and infected communities wherever she went, while never becoming ill herself. She is what is called an asymptomatic carrier. Ultimately, American authorities were forced to quarantine her as a public menace.

So who are the asymptomatic carriers of psychic epidemics in American politics—the people who have turned American against American, and paralyzed our governments at the local, state and national levels? Do they rise to the level of terrorists, who try to destroy the American system intentionally? Are they the Koch Brothers, those infamous sons one of the founders of the John Birch Society? Is the feckless television commentator, who insisted that Santa Claus is white an asymptomatic carrier? Well, Santa probably is white for her, but Santa Claus is a myth with no intrinsic color, and with origins decidedly Middle Eastern, just like Jesus Christ. But the controversy was used by many cable channels to distract attention from the fact that the federal government (both houses of Congress and the President) passed the National Defense Authorization Act (S. 1867), which continues the probably unconstitutional provision for the arrest and indefinite detention of American citizens without a warrant. Who was responsible for that? Whisper who dares!

While everyone was worried about the race of a myth, our government agreed to curtail a basic right of American citizens. What's next?! Justifications like those that followed the Berlin Reichstag Fire of February 27, 1933 come immediately to mind. The Reichstag Fire Decree was one of the main cornerstones of the Nazis curtailing civil rights of German citizens and taking over the German government, making Adolph Hitler a dictator leading one of the most horrific psychic epidemics of all time.

What about fundamentalist preachers and priests, who have stoked the fires of the social issues? What about you? Are you an asymptomatic carrier of a psychic epidemic? Examine thyself! If we get the wrong answer, the consequences are pretty monumental for the American people and the people of the world.

Chapter 37: The Tea Party: The Beginning of the End

"You want to be a missionary?
You got that missionary zeal?
Let somebody change your life;
How's that make you feel."
Paul Simon, "Hurricane's Eye"

When Arizona Governor Jan Brewer vetoed Senate Bill 1062 on February 26, 2014, I knew that we had seen the beginning of the end of the Tea Party. That was the bill in the Arizona legislature, which many believed would allow businesses to discriminate against the LGBT community.

Governor Brewer is known for her conservative views, and much of her support has come from The Tea Party wing of the Republican Party. The veto is an example of the type of political acts President John F. Kennedy referred to in his Pulitzer Prize winning book, *Profiles in Courage*. Governor Brewer had to deny one of the most cherished ideals of The Tea Party, and thereby lost the support of many who had put her in office.

She had to dig into the depths of her own Soul, and make the right decision for all of her constituents, the people of Arizona, not just her right wing cronies. She earned my respect as a leader. Decisions like this are what American political leadership is all about. We do not have to always agree with a politician to support their performance of their duty in office. When we elect someone in the United States, we are choosing someone to be our representative to make the right decision for all of their constituents, not only the cabal that put them in power.

Of course, it is human nature to want one's own way in life. We see this in the temper tantrums of infants, who cry because they don't get their way. The world is filled with little tyrants, who run companies and organizations, and who have adopted the motto "my way or the highway" to reflect their leadership style. But, like anything, there are bounds; limits beyond which we cannot go without forfeiting some of the virtues that have given strength to The United States of America.

Dr. Carl G. Jung wrote for more than six decades about the factors which give energy to life. He pointed out that all of the movement in life comes from the energy that arises between two extremes. He spoke of the top and the bottom of a cliff as two extremes, and the water running between them as a metaphor for the energy. In this example, the energy flows in only one direction, but he went on to point out that energy flows in both directions at different times and in different ways, or nothing happens.

The metaphor applies to politics too. For a time, it seems the energy can flow in only one direction, and the "my way or the highway" people of The Tea Party are like that. They think they can dictate to the rest of us how we should live. This is contrary to the spirit of The United States, which was founded in large part by normal people, who were trying to escape that style of leadership. But one man's idea is another man's anathema, and the strength of our country comes from the process of vigorous and respectful debate, which winnows out bad ideas and allows good ideas to float to the surface.

Our national spirit has been roiled by the turbulence caused by the 9/11 attacks. Such an extreme event naturally engenders an opposite reaction from those who are attacked. The Tea Party was conceived in that environment. Because religious intolerance was involved, it was natural for religious absolutism to respond reciprocally, and start to follow the "my way or the highway" path. This in turn attracted a lot of unconscious angst, which had floated in the deep unconscious of our nation since The Civil War.

Whenever a major cataclysm occurs, regardless of origin and outcome, society has to find an adaptation, which will allow it to find a steady state in its societal psyche, and allow it to perform as a society once again. After The Civil War, there was naturally a lot of underlying resentment, on both the winning and losing sides. On both sides, the loss of the blossom of a generation was deeply felt. But, like a neurosis, which puts one's psyche in turmoil, people had to cordon off that resentment and adapt to a single American nation reborn.

But major events can open old wounds in unpredictable ways, and a new adaptation must be found. The political polarization we are experiencing in the United States right now is a manifestation of this reopening of old wounds. They had scabbed over and were healing in many ways, but events worked to allow our demons to run for the extremes once again. The Tea Party was one manifestation of this natural human phenomenon. It was an experiment in how far the conservative point of view could reassert itself in American society. By her veto, Governor Brewer has said, "This far, and no farther."

One of the major psychic phenomena, which Dr. Jung discussed in his long career of prodigious scholarship, was the idea of enantiodromia. That is the tendency of things in the extreme to turn into their opposite. One of the interesting errors that has surfaced recently is that because Abraham Lincoln was a Republican, he was a conservative. This is not true by any stretch of the imagination. If that were true, he would have left slavery in place in the South, as many wanted him to do. Even the Founding Fathers of our country called slavery "The Wolf," and knew the issue had the potential to devour the nation, which it very nearly did.

The switch of the Republican Party from a party that advanced the end of slavery to a party that espouses new forms of "Jim Crow" laws in the South is a perfect example of enantiodromia. Many of us are old enough to remember that the party of intolerance and bigotry in the South was the Democratic Party. It was the party of George Wallace, Lester Maddox, Harry F. Byrd, Sr. and James Lindsey Almond, Jr. My how times have changed!

These massive changes in our country's psyche are only examples of how enantiodromia works in politics. Governor Jan Brewer's courageous decision to veto Senate Bill 1062 is a symptom of this same phenomenon at work on our polarized politics right now. It is a sign that we have seen the beginning of the end of The Tea Party, and there is nothing that the Koch brothers or any of the other powers that be can do about it. Buh bye!

Chapter 38: How Are the Oligarchs Getting Paid Twice on Our Mortgages?

During the last decade, the Oligarchs of the United States have performed the largest public theft in the history of history. Tens of millions of Americans have lost their life's savings, because the American Oligarchy was allowed to add risk on risk until they crashed the economy, all the time paying themselves $100 million annual bonuses. That was pretty good for them, don't you think? Did you ever wonder how any individual was worth that much money?

When the crash came, they simply told a bunch of economically unsophisticated Congressmen that they were "too big to fail," and they would have to be bailed out. It wasn't hard to put that one over on President George W. Bush, who was always a part of the Oligarchy in the first place.

The result was that while the housing market crashed, the Oligarchy was all right. Decisions were made in hours or days, which should have been thoroughly debated. But Henry Paulson, former Chairman of Goldman Sachs, was Secretary of the Treasury, and he knew what would be best for the Oligarchy.

When the housing market crashed, because of their risk shenanigans, it wasn't hard to blame average Americans. We've dumbed down our educational system to the point that the average American can barely check out at the super market, so they could hardly be faulted for failing to understand what was happening.

When all of our bad mortgages were paid off by credit default swaps and other mechanisms, the costs of which were foisted on us by the Oligarchy in the form of bailouts, they never bothered to tell the rest of us that our defaulted mortgage debt had been paid off. As a result of that, the Oligarchy got paid on the mortgages by the government bailouts, and then they got paid **A SECOND TIME** by unsuspecting homeowners, who felt guilty because they could no longer pay when they lost their jobs in the economic catastrophe. They simply decided to turn over their homes to the banks, either by turning in their keys or by allowing foreclosures to go unchallenged. What a scam!

And now they're trying to do it again. They don't want the economy to get better very fast. Yes, it's partially because they don't want the Democrats to look good, but it is also because they want the economy crammed down as much as possible, so that they can ride it up again for the next 20-30 years. They don't care what's good for the average American, they only care about where they can hide their $100 million bonuses from taxation; and how they can fleece unsuspecting foreigners, who think that money invested in U.S. dollars is safe, even if it's invested in inflated financial instruments.

I don't doubt that when he began running for office, President Barack Obama was as altruistic as the best traditions of the average American. But it's very clear that he has been co-opted and controlled by the Oligarchy. Results speak for themselves! Even though we've all been fleeced by the 1%, he has really done nothing to prosecute the Oligarchs, who committed massive fraud; who socialized risk but privatized profits; who had their losses covered by the federal government; and who are now in the process of collecting a second time by taking all of our homes and life's savings improperly.

Oh yes, there was the three ring show trial of the sacrificial Sri Lankan American investment banker, Raj Rajaratnam, but he was simply the sacrificial brown face used to take the spotlight off of what the Oligarchs did. There have been a couple of other minor examples, and Bernie Madoff, but they're really bit players compared to what's really been going on   .

Do you think the mainstream "investigative reporters" will ever cover this on your television on 60 Minutes, CNN, MSNBC, or the Evening News? Not bloody likely, because they all depend for their rice bowls on the Oligarchs. No, if anything will ever be done about the injustices that have been done to the average American over the last five years, we will all have to do it ourselves.

Full disclosure here: I am one of the Americans that lost big in the financial collapse. The bank is currently trying to foreclose for the second time. The first time around I fought them off by representing myself. This time I had a forensic report completed, which says, among other things, that the debt is probably not even in default, because it was covered by a credit default swap years ago. And the cost of that was covered by the bailouts. Who do I owe? How would I know? Of course, no one will tell me the truth, because to do so would be to reveal the truth of this colossal rip off of the American people.

If the Oligarchy should be saved by the bailouts, why shouldn't the average American be saved? Why should the Oligarchs get paid twice, and because of their own profligate behavior with the economy? Why should tens of millions of average Americans lose their life's savings, simply because they are ignorant of what the real deals were in the halls of power?

I thought my government was supposed to protect me from that sort of behavior. Ah, but that was in a time long, long ago, in a universe far from here. Now it is the privileged class that has control, and which is rapidly installing a new kind of Feudalism in the economic life of our planet.

The movie "Elysium", which opens in August, explores the long-term consequences of allowing the Oligarchy to continue to control our lives in this pernicious way. Pay attention!

This video can be found on Youtube as "ELYSIUM - Official HD Trailer #2"

Chapter 39: A Modest Proposal to Save the Middle Class

The American Middle Class is being crammed down by inaction in Washington and unregulated Wall Street. Banks are conspiring with real estate brokers and appraisers to reduce pricing in the housing market, thereby destroying a major component of the life's savings of many Americans—their home. The 1% wants this process to continue, because once they cram down the Middle Class, they have what amounts to a "reset" of the economy at a much lower level, and they can ride it up again, much as they rode it up over the last half of the Twentieth Century.

There's a serious problem with government allowing banks to do this, and there is a simple solution. The problem is that we were called upon to "bail them out," on short notice with very little debate, and now we're being called upon to allow this reset of the economy, which is crushing the savings of the Middle Class by destroying our home values and forcing about 10 million families into foreclosures—many of which are being fraudulently pursued.

Our home was recently "appraised" at 41.5% of the value it was "appraised" for in 2004. That is ridiculous! Nothing changed about the value of our home over the intervening time, except that appraisers know that bankers want the real estate market "reset" at this lower pricing level. Real estate brokers are playing along, because they need income.

The solution is quite simple. We need to reset the value of all of the mortgages on the books of the banks.
In our case, if our house is to be valued at 41.5% of its previous value, then let our mortgage also be reset at 41.5% of its previous value. If this were done across the board, it would have no impact on the real financial health of any of the banks, but it would be much fairer for the Middle Class. This proposal

would amount to a bookkeeping entry that would not hurt the banks the Middle Class saved from collapse. Since all banks would be required to comply, this proposal would save some of the equity that has evaporated from the Middle Class, without causing a further financial crisis.

The Middle Class was required to save the banks from collapse with no warning, and after a bare minimum of debate. President Bush and Treasury Secretary Paulson simply told Congress it had to be done or else. Now the Middle Class is being crushed by the consequences. How is that fair? The way things stand right now, we've bailed out the banks, and now the government is allowing them to pick our pockets and reset the economy so they can do it again over the next 20 or 30 years.

This suggestion would save millions of homes from foreclosure, put money back into the retirement savings of the Middle Class, and give us confidence in our government processes once again. I can hear the responses to this on Wall Street now! But this is the only fair response to a truly unfair set of circumstances that Wall Street created.

If conservative pundits want to know why Middle Class Americans are in the streets in outrage, this is why! We saved the banks; they continued to pay themselves huge bonuses with our money, while their companies were insolvent; and now they want to destroy our life's savings so they can do it again. We need a bailout too! A solution like this is the only fair thing to do. We are the 99% and we want government to look out for us the way it looked out for Wall Street!

Chapter 40: Why the Super Rich Don't Want You to Understand Investment

When the Super Rich, like Mitt Romney, talk about investment creating jobs, they are hoping the listener will not differentiate among types of investment. The reason is that while some investments do in fact create jobs, others are just gambling, with stakes higher than allowed in casinos, and do not deserve special treatment in taxes.

Very broadly speaking there are three types of investment: 1) small business startups; 2) traditional stock market investment; and 3) casino style derivatives investment and other esoteric investments.

1. Small Business Startups:
The type of investment that produces jobs is the investment that small entrepreneurs put into their companies to get things going. Obviously, the very first thing a new company invests in is people to give it life, so this type of investment does produce jobs. We can include in this so-called "Angel Investors", who invest at a very early stage in a company's life, and risk losing all of their money if a new company fails, which happens often. Studies vary, but a variety of studies say that about 33% of all new businesses have failed because of performance within the first four years.

Since government wants to encourage new businesses, which are the most likely to create new jobs in our economy, it does make sense to give a low income tax rate on capital gains to this type of investment.

2. Traditional Stock Market Investment:
When you invest in a common share on the New York Stock Exchange or NASDAQ, normally no jobs are created. The only exception to this rule is when

there is an "initial public offering." In this latter case, the money you invest goes directly to the company, after the Wizards of Wall Street take their pound of flesh, so the money can be used to expand the company and create jobs in various ways. In all other cases, though, the company in which you are investing gets absolutely none of the money. The share ownership has already been distributed among shareholders at the "initial public offering," so you are simply exchanging these shares with someone else, who may or may not have put money into the company at the time the money actually went to the company.

Government should want to encourage this type of investment as well, because it is where many of our pension funds reside and because the total size and liquidity of the market encourages people to make the Type 1 "angel investments" above. In this case, some lower income tax on capital gains still seems appropriate, though perhaps not as much as Type 1 investment, where the risk is much greater.

3. Casino Style Derivatives Trading and Other Esoteric Investments:
What we should surely be taxing at ordinary income rates is income from financial instruments that produce neither jobs, nor anything at all. These are Derivatives, which are financial tools of either insurance or speculation. The Internal Revenue Service surely gets its pound of flesh from the "Let It Ride" lucky gambler in Las Vegas, but it treats Wall Street "investors" in derivatives (read "gamblers") as if they are job creators. They are not!

Let us take a few examples. A credit default swap is an insurance policy that guarantees a debtor will pay its bill. When the debt is paid, the premium paid becomes income to the party that wrote the insurance. But, under current tax rules, that income is often treated as long-term capital gain, taxed at the very lowest rates. We all remember how AIG socialized risk when it forced the American people to pay its shortfalls when too many debts failed in 2008. But AIG is not paying taxes that justify having the American people take that unexpected and un-negotiated risk.

Commodities contracts are another good example. It used to be that when you bought a Winter Wheat contract, you were buying the right to a railroad train carload of Winter Wheat for delivery on a certain day, thus supporting American farmers. If you held onto the contract, you would by-and-by get a call from the railroad siding saying, "I have your carload of Winter Wheat, where do you want it?" That is no longer true. Now you are only buying a contract that is based on the value of a carload of Winter Wheat, but there could be 100 or more such contracts sold on the same carload of Winter Wheat. The business of buying and selling these contracts therefore has no more substance to it than playing Black Jack with 52 playing cards.

The only reason the financial industry gets away with the commodities market and other derivatives is because they control the language. They call what they are doing "investing" even though it is no less gambling than Poker.

Suffice it to say that any financial activity that is not directly related to the production of jobs should not be allowed "capital gains" tax rates. "Capital gains" rates were about giving investors a return for putting their money at risk in the economy to increase the economy as a whole—job creation. They were not established to keep gamblers free from tax, regardless of what we happen to call them this week.

Chapter 41: Breaking the Grover Norquist Pledge

As the story goes, Grover Norquist spent much of the 1990s going around the country getting politicians and wannabees to sign his pledge that they would never raise taxes under any circumstances. In the current election cycle, he seems to have many of these candidates under his thumb, and some pundits have called him the most powerful man in American. It's time to break the hold this and any other pledge has over our politicians. We should be demanding that every politician assert that he has made no pledge whatsoever prior to taking office, and his or her only pledge relating to their behavior in office is their Oath of Office.

Why do I say this so emphatically? Times change; situations change. When we elect a candidate to represent us in Congress, as President, or in any other role, it means that they are going into that office to represent what is best for their constituency—100% of it! If they've taken a pledge like Mr. Norquist's, then they have sworn to only represent the interests of those behind the pledge, come what may. What if the situation changes?

I, for one, don't want to support any candidate who refuses to listen to the debate about how things should be. If they are not going to consider all of the circumstances when a matter comes up for a vote, then I don't want that person representing me.

Of course, I do agree that candidates should state their general positions on as many issues as they can, but I never want them to have already promised how they will vote on an issue without first listening to all arguments and considering them in terms of what is best for their entire constituency at the time of the vote.

It is surely too late to change things for this election cycle, but as we move forward, let us demand pledges from all candidates that they have not and will not be bound by any pledge except their oath to uphold and defend

The Constitution of the United States. Only then can we be sure that this person represents their entire constituency when debates arise on issues.

Chapter 42: Democrats and Media Are Dupes of the Tea Party or Dopes

"It is the opposite which is good for us." --
Heraclitus (cited by C.G.Jung and Paul M. Wortman, PhD)

Words matter! This article is about a Tea Party buzzword, "ObamaCare". It is incredibly stupid to adopt the political buzzwords of your opponent; and if you are the media, you must give up all pretense of fundamental fairness if you adopt the buzzwords of any political party.

"ObamaCare" is the topic of the day, so let's start there. Ever since The Affordable Care Act was enacted in March 2010, the so-called "Tea Party" has labeled it "ObamaCare", with a view to hanging it around the neck of The President of the United States as an albatross. Ironically, The President had very little to do with the cause of assuring affordable healthcare for all Americans, which has been a goal of many for the best part of a century.

By beating on the "ObamaCare" theme day in and day out, the Tea Party was successful in getting many Democrats and all of the mainstream media to begin using the term. This strategy has worked for the Tea Party in remarkable ways, as the following video plainly shows:

This video can be found on Youtube as
"Six of One - Obamacare vs. The Affordable Care Act"

Obviously, if you favor the Tea Party, you have to think this strategy is a wonderful success. But there is a double-edged sword! Many, including Dr. Jung, have said, "Words are like wild animals." They take on a life of their own. In the fullness of time, thanks to the constant harping of the Tea Party and Republicans generally, we may see one of Dr. Jung's other principles come into play. That is the concept of *"enantiodromia,"* which says that things tend to turn into their opposite.

At this point of time, we would have to say that "ObamaCare" has a negative connotation as a reference to The Affordable Care Act, as the video demonstrates clearly. But, now that the new healthcare exchanges are in operation, Americans may very well find that they like it, and "ObamaCare" may become a kind of monument to the success of President Obama's time in office.

Even *The Wall Street Journal*, in "Obamacare—A Game-Changer in the Making? ", acknowledged on October 2, 2013 that it might turn out to be a good thing. Speaking for myself, I knew the Tea Party had lost the "ObamaCare" fight a couple of weeks back, when I heard that IBM has adopted it for its retirees, and even Walmart has jumped aboard. Author David Wessel also mentions Walgreen Co., Sears Holdings Corp., and Darden Restaurants Inc. as early adopters. The sand is clearly melting from beneath the feet of the Tea Party stalwarts, who have been standing their ground.

Dr. Jung's enantiodromia point about the opposites was not that one side or the other ever is correct, but that the tension between them creates the energy for a "third thing" to be developed—namely, a compromise. I do not mean by this that any part of "ObamaCare" should be changed, although I acknowledge that many of us would agree that parts of it will not stand up to scrutiny, if taken one by one. That is a process that should evolve in due course. What I mean is that Congress can and will find a middle ground "third thing" vis-a-vis the budget debate and the debt ceiling, which will allow the government to perform its role once again, including paying its bills in a timely fashion.

As for me, I'll be honoring "ObamaCare" as one of the crowning achievements of the Obama Administration, and as a suitable epitaph for the John Birch Society political-movement-in-sheep's-clothing known as the "Tea Party". "ObamaCare is the rock on which the 'Tea Party' was broken. RIP."

The War on Women

Chapter 43: Why Will Women Change the Map from Red to Blue?

The biggest underlying question in Political Psychology relates to what a party must do to change the opinion of its opponent's supporters. The answer is that people have to know the truth for themselves, and no amount of debate on television can change that fundamental fact. It is virtually impossible to change minds based on the polarized political polemic we see from the talking heads on television these days.

Holding a political position is based on experience. No rational argument is going to change someone's mind when they **know** better   .

Offensive behavior and name calling are even less likely to give someone political success. Did you ever vote for the school yard bully when he ran for class President?

This is why the Republican Party and the Tea Party have already lost the women's vote, and may not be able to gain it back for a generation. Deep down inside, more and more women know that the best interests of their daughters will not be served by the Republican Party. Regardless of what they may say to their husbands to keep peace at home, women have the right to vote privately and silently, and they will carry the future with them.

On her deathbed, my mother felt it was important to tell me that in 1960 she voted for John F. Kennedy, despite the fact that my Navy father was sure that Richard Nixon was the right man, and my bigoted grandfather couldn't say enough offensive things about Mr. Kennedy's religion. That was a secret she could easily have carried into the hereafter, but something in her unconscious wanted to tell the secret; to say that she too had lived and made her own decision.

Sometimes it is difficult to express what your experience tells you is true, even though you **know** the truth. The dilemma of "Contact" character Dr. Ellie Arroway (Jodie Foster) shows this point clearly. After a movie full of the buildup of putting together a machine, which would do something, no one knew what, Dr. Arroway was selected to have the experience. In the event, though, it appeared to everyone outside of the machine that the experiment was a failure. While Dr. Arroway did have an 18-hour experience, to everyone outside it appeared that nothing whatever happened, and only a few seconds had passed. Later, when testifying before Congress, she could not convince her rivals that something had happened, but she knew what she knew:

This video can be found on Youtube as "I had an experience"

Something about our age has given men of the patriarchal Tea Party and Republican Party license to tell women to sit down and shut up, to condone rape, and to obstruct laws against domestic violence. These misogynists don't represent the majority any longer, and they will only "get it" when women have turned the map from red to blue.

Women have always represented the subtle tide of change, and their instincts point in a progressive direction. If they live in red states, the majority of women may have to toe the mark of a patriarchal household, as women did a century ago. But when they are in the polling station they are answerable only to themselves, and they **know what to do!**

Chapter 44: Republican War on Women Is a Manifestation of Evil

The despicable Republican candidates, who want to **redefine** RAPE so that their pubescent sons can get away with raping pubescent women, are very simply manifestations of the Devil!
Today I was criticized by a Republican woman, who characterized the Republican War on Women as something created by liberals to deflect from what is really going on. That's the Republican narrative, and she's stickin' to it! The Truth is that the Republican War on Women is so broad and deep, that **it simply must be stopped!**

The War on Women has been on for decades, with Republicans chipping away at Women's Rights at the State and local level, to the tune of 1,100 bills last year. The Republican Congress passed 44 bills on abortion and ZERO on job creation, not to mention 36 bills on marriage and 71 on family relationships. They clearly want government out of business, but in your personal life big time!

This morning (October 24, 2012) I woke up to the news that Richard Mourdock (R-Indiana) has gone on record as saying he would only support abortion when the life of the Mother was at stake, and that a pregnancy resulting from a RAPE was a "gift from God." If you believe that, Richard, then you too deserve to be called a manifestation of the Devil for saying so. Such a pregnancy is quite simply a **Curse from the Devil.** To suggest that a woman would have to see her RAPIST in the eyes of her child is surely a lifetime condemnation to HELL for an innocent VICTIM.

If a woman in your life were raped with the threat that their nipples would be cut off with a knife if they did not comply, how would you react? Should those rapists have paternal rights?! The very idea of it makes me want to spit! The Republicans that have been casually talking about such things are despicable beyond words, and women need to make sure that they are banished from office, even if the men won't do it. What Father accepts that his Grandchild is the child of such a rapist? Good grief! What kind of a man is he?

Republicans have been using the abortion issue as a divisive emotional wedge to suck in unsuspecting young women, who do not understand the EVIL that permeated society before Roe v. Wade. This EVIL is addressed in two popular movies, "In the Heat of the Night" and "Dirty Dancing". Republicans know very well that banning abortion will not stop abortion nor even slow it down, because we have our own experiences in this country to prove what happens. Not a single baby will be saved.

Abortion is not an easy issue. I am not in favor of it in my personal life. Nonetheless, I know the consequences to society if abortion is illegal. It is true that medical doctors prior to 1972 performed many abortions, but they were committing felonies. **What does it mean when we criminalize our medical profession?**

More importantly, the psychological impact on women having abortions is always immeasurable, even when the procedure is done legally. Governor McDonnell of Virginia wants to shame women with trans-vaginal ultrasounds. But what does that accomplish? Don't women who have abortions have to deal with enough shame, without the government piling on and making it worse?

My Mother, on her deathbed, told me two things that she wanted to be sure I knew. One was that **my two GrandMothers had 5 abortions between them in the 1920s.** This was a stunning revelation to me, because both of these women were paragons of the Victorian Era, as far as I knew. But they experienced their youth at a time when birth control devices were haphazard, even for married women, so they must have felt compelled to control their family size. To think these two women would feel compelled to commit felonies is truly beyond my imagination, but nevertheless, this is so. Ask your GrandMothers what the truth was in their time! If they are willing to tell you, you may be surprised by the answers you receive. My Mother also wanted me to put two and two together, I think, so that I would understand how courageous she truly was. You see, my Mother was 19 when she became pregnant with me. My parents had a cover story that they maintained for 50 years, which was that they were married on my Father's birthday, which would have been 10 months before I was born. The truth only officially emerged when I was invited to their 50th Anniversary party, celebrating a date that was only 7 months before I was born.

One can only imagine the pressures my Mother must have experienced from my GrandMothers in deciding whether to give birth to me. I never doubted my Mother's courage in any case, but I know that she would very much have appreciated the rights to contraception that young women have today, and which Republicans are trying to restrict.

My Mother's second revelation was that in 1960 she voted for President John F. Kennedy, even though my Father believed until his death that she voted with him for Richard Nixon. The beauty of a voting booth is that it is individual, and women do not need to vote with their husbands, and no one needs to know!

Election 2012 has been a divisive one in American history. It seems to me the issues of Women's Rights are extremely serious in this election. Our Grand-Mothers will roll over in their graves if women give up their rights after such hard and continuing struggles that women continue to have to face in life.

This video can be found on Youtube as GOP Rep Says No Abortion Exceptions For Health of Mother

Chapter 45: Rush Limbaugh and a Failure of Courage in the American Psyche

We, who take exception to Rush Limbaugh's antics about women and Women's Rights, might want to pity him and his listeners instead. They may certainly deserve our pity. Based on my analysis, which follows, they may be Momma's boys, who have failed a critical step in individuation (the steps that lead to our psychological maturity as human beings). This failure may mean a failure to develop the courage necessary to face the world as it is.

All of us amount to a mass of "projections" in the psychological sense. When we hate something, it is often more true that we hate some subconscious aspect of ourselves and we project it upon another. Yes, it is true that those of us who detest the Republican War on Women are projecting something onto the perpetrators of that war. But, it is also true that they are projecting something out onto society at large, and sometimes such projections become a "Thing" that is bad for society at large. **It is best to understand why Rush Limbaugh is as he is.**

All of us are probably familiar with the passages of life. Those are the psychological steps one must take to move from one stage to the next. Dr. Carl Jung described "libido" as the life force (rather than something that is only and specifically sexual). He explained that in the first half of life, the libido is seeking to extrovert by exercising its courage, by moving away from the womb to mature and live in the world at large; and in the second half of life we are introverting toward the more spiritual aspects of being—we are seeking to return to the womb psychologically by imagining that we will be in some perfect Elysium after our deaths. He called this psychological process individuation.

One of the most important psychological steps is breaking away from the Mother. Traditionally this was an act of courage, and is expressed as the hero's fight with the dragon (the Mother) in mythology. When the hero wins this fight, he gets the beautiful damsel or the treasure of great value. This means that he has earned his right to mature manhood in society. He or she has slain the Dragon (of his subconscious instinct to want to return to the security of Mother), and displayed his or her courage and, therefore, the right to move into society as a mature human being.

We often see this psychological contest played out on movie screens. Indeed, in "Alien" Sigourney Weaver fought the horrible alien monster and even called her a "bitch". But that ugly creature is there in the subconscious of each of us and, if we do not win the battle, we may regress back toward the infantile. We see this everywhere in American society, where 30 something men have failed to take the necessary steps to break away from the security of their parental home.

Rush Limbaugh's outrages toward women are only the same drama played out for his listeners. He attacks women (either insidiously because he knows this or because he hasn't outgrown his own Mother) as surrogates for attacking his Mother. His subconscious needs to do this because it seems evident from his personal life that he has been unable to have a mature relationship with women—four wives. So his attacks are psychologically attacks on this dragon in his subconscious. He is actually displaying for all to see his failure to mature to a point where he can actually have a mature relationship with a fully mature woman. That would be courageous, but he evidently cannot achieve that, so his struggle plays out on his radio program day in and day out when he talks about women.

Limbaugh's listeners, on the other hand, are also projecting, but they are projecting their dragons onto Limbaugh's battle, rather than face that battle internally, in their own psyches. In other words, their psyche has not produced the courage necessary to break away from their urge to return to the protection of their Mothers, so they pretend they are doing it by watching Limbaugh's battle. Their psyche then pretends that they have won the battle, but they have really achieved nothing in their actual life.

Thinking about this in another way, male individuation requires us to display enough courage to become warriors. But most American men, instead of actually becoming warriors become armchair warriors by watching sports on television every week. These mythic battles may seem important (to the psyche and its projected needs), but they actually accomplish nothing in the real life of the viewer. This is not true for the players themselves, who actually are entering onto a physical field of battle. They are actually demonstrating their courage and their right to claim that they are mature men in society entitled to the prizes to which their prowess may entitle them.

So it is that many women live in a world where their men have failed to meet their true mature responsibilities, because they have fulfilled their psychic needs for individuation through projection, rather than through their own deeds. This leads to all kinds of problems in society. Men become angry with their wives, for example, because they have not behaved like their Mothers in fulfilling all of their needs, thus resulting in a greater than 40% divorce rate in the United States.

I would suggest that mature men, who have the courage to pass the necessary step of breaking away from their Mothers in their real life, instead of in their pretend life with Rush Limbaugh, will respect there wives more completely as mature women, and find the courage to resolve differences that are inevitable in a marriage. This requires no religious stricture to implement. It only requires an autonomous morality that is potential in each of us.

So, the next time you meet someone, who thinks Rush Limbaugh's and Republican attacks on women are just right, have a thought for them. They may require your sympathy, because they may be miserable in their subconscious minds. They may not have the courage to live a full and satisfying life.

Chapter 46: What Kind of a Man Are You?

There have been a lot of heated words in this election season, so there is just one question I want to ask my fellow men, who still plan to vote for Republican candidates. What kind of MAN are you?

Let's peel away all of the other issues, which have been thrown around in this election campaign, and talk about the one that truly puts YOUR MANHOOD on the line. That is the one where certain Republican candidates have suggested that RAPE should be redefined.

That attitude is one that will invite men to RAPE women, believing they can get away with it. What about you? Do you want your high school age son to think that he can pull down a girl classmate and rape her? If you are the Father of daughters, would you want men to think it is OK to rape, or that they can get away with it?

If your Mother, Wife, or Daughter is raped, but there are inadequate laws to prosecute the rapist, even though you know who the rapist is, what will you do? What will you do when you see that man on the street? How will you behave when that man comes to your door and wants visitation rights with the child he has fathered in the rape of your daughter?

Christian values have been used in many ways in this election season, but I want to know: Do you believe that EVIL exists in the world? Would you see the face of the DEVIL in the face of your Wife's rapist? Would you stand up for this rapists paternity visitation rights if he impregnated your wife? What would you do?

Nothing much is going to change in the United States after this election campaign. Come what may, we will have a deadlocked Senate, regardless of which party has a majority, so neither party is going to be able to move hugely ideological pieces of legislation, because they will be stopped. Only compromise will win the day in Congress.

But legitimizing the idea that RAPE is OK in our society is very dangerous. If you believe the positions of these extreme Republican candidates is OK, how do you claim that you are conservative?

Leaving all other issues aside, it seems to me that all men of moral virtue must draw a line in the sand on this one. As you raise your sons and daughters, how will you educate them about their moral responsibility? Are you the kind of man that thinks it's OK for your son to drag a young woman under the bleachers and rape her? If that's the case, you might want to re-evaluate why you are wasting your time going to church on Sunday.

Five years from now, or forty years from now, when you look yourself in the mirror after a woman in your life has been raped, how will you feel about your vote this year? Will you be OK with the idea that you allowed the firewall against rape to be eviscerated? Will you be proud of your vote for Todd Akin, Richard Mourdock, Joe Walsh, and Paul Ryan? If so, WHAT KIND OF A MAN ARE YOU?

Chapter 47: It's the Social Contract Stupid

Conservative pundits are busy whistling in the wind, arguing that the Occupy Wall Street Movement has no objectives, no common complaints, and worst of all, no leader! They've been hoping that the American people would believe them when they keep trying to argue that the demonstrations springing up around the world are a group of bongo playing hippies. The mainstream media has gone out of its way to show participants from the fringes of society, because their pocket book wielding masters don't want the rest of us to catch on that the movement is really coming from people just like us. Oops! Too late! We're the 99%!

The reason the Occupy Movement is going viral is very simple: The "Social Contract" is severely broken. The second half of the 20th Century was relatively comfortable for most living Americans. After years of war and depression, the powerful focused their attention on building the American economy. This meant huge growth for the economy, and opportunity for all. Americans could grow up in relative comfort, be educated, go to work, raise families, and die with a modicum of dignity.

So why are people suddenly in the streets, like the French Revolution? The answer is summed up by the famous French quote from that time, "Let them eat cake." It reflected the fact that one of the French princesses, who apocryphally uttered this phrase, was totally out of touch with the conditions faced by her people. So it is with the 1% "Masters of the Universe", who have infamously overstepped their powers and rights, and brought Americans into the streets in great and growing numbers.

Most of us are looking around and saying, "What ever happened to all of these things we were promised, earned and were expecting, but now seem to be evaporating before our eyes?" In my case, those things are simple. I invested heavily in my home, so that my wife and I could be comfortable in our retirement. I served 23 years in the U.S. Marine Corps and U.S. Marine Corps Reserve, so that we would have a small pension and health insurance in our old age. I had great pride about the Rights all Americans enjoyed thanks to the First Amendment of the U.S. Constitution.

But what do I have? A house "appraised" at 41.5% of its "appraised" value in 2004. Its value in supporting our retirement is gone with the wind. A Republican Congress that seems intent on reducing the health insurance benefit, which I already earned for my military service, and to squeeze my small pension by not allowing it to keep up with the rate of inflation. The health insurance was converted to Medicare during the Reagan Administration, and now they are cutting payments to doctors so badly that most doctors won't accept Medicare. That's the backhanded way to steal my earned healthcare benefit and Medicare in general. And then there's the series of politicians across the United States (I won't call them public servants), who think it's OK to ignore our Constitutional Right of Assembly and our Constitutional Right to Petition the Government for Redress of Grievances. Who are these people anyway?

I often say that America's Diversity is the Glory of God, and the one factor above all others that has consistently contributed to making The United States of America the envy of the world. As Winston Churchill famously put it:

"Americans can always be counted on to do the righ thing...after they have exhausted all other possibilities."

So it is that when good ideas emerge from any of our thousands of interest groups, we all adopt them. But when bad ideas emerge, we all shout and argue, and sometimes fight, until the bad ideas are pushed out of the system.

The "Masters of the Universe" thought "trickle down" economics was the right way to go. They thought it was perfectly fine to pay themselves $100 million annual bonuses, at the expense of their shareholders. They thought that adding financial leverage on financial leverage was perfectly fine to grow their wealth. Even famous economists like Alan Greenspan thought that their profligacy could go on forever. They were wrong! That's why people are in the streets now!

Most of us have been feeling the pinch for decades. Oh, it wasn't that much at first, and it was only a little bit at a time, but the prosperity of our parents has been taken away for us. The Occupy Movement is only a way of saying that the "tipping point" has been reached, and now it's our turn to set the rules. The Occupy Movement is not going to dissipate until a new "Social Contract" is written for everyone!

Thank heaven for Scott Walker, temporarily the Governor of Wisconsin. His infamous over reach against collective bargaining rights in Wisconsin has awakened all Americans to the fact that the "class warfare" the rich are now complaining of has been going on for 30 years. The rich are only now feeling the pinch because the American people are in the streets telling them, "Enough!"

Chapter 48: 10 Ways the Social Contract Is Broken

Jean-Jacques Rousseau described the "Social Contract" in his 1762 treatise as follows:

> *The heart of the idea of the social contract may be stated simply: Each of us places his person and authority under the supreme direction of the general will, and the group receives each individual as an indivisible part of the whole...*

By this he meant that there are certain unwritten understandings by which everyone in a society operates. These can be changed, but as the French and American Revolutions and the Arab Spring have shown us, often only with significant upheaval. These changes often occur when the majority finally says to the powers that be that the status quo in the society is not good enough.

We have reached such a time in the United States of America. Bill Moyers quotes The Radicalism of the American Revolution by Gordon Wood:

> *"... our nation discovered its greatness "by creating a prosperous free society belonging to obscure people with their workaday concerns and pecuniary pursuits of happiness." This democracy, he said, changed the lives of "hitherto neglected and despised masses of common laboring people."*

Unfortunately, the 1% of our population controlling 50% of our economy have turned away or forgotten this. In his article **"How Wall Street Occupied America,"** found in the November 21, 2011 edition of The Nation, he points to a confidential memorandum published by former Supreme Court Justice Lewis

Powell among his friends at the U.S. Chamber of Commerce on August 23, 1971. Moyers says, **"We look on it now as a call to arms for class war waged from the top down."**

It is warfare waged successfully and largely unnoticed by the Middle Class. Like the frog, which dies in a pot growing steadily warmer, the American people have had too many distractions to notice the heat rising on the American Dream. Most of these distractions provided happily by the 1%. Like the Caesars before them, they allowed us great spectacles like the National Football League and interminable sex scandals on television, part of the television wasteland, and they provided us with foreign wars to make us afraid to complain.

But, like the frog that jumps out of the pot when the heat rises too quickly, the Occupy Movement represents the American People's response to the fact that the 1% has literally gone too far. In 2011, the early signs of this discontent have come because of over reaching political attacks on collective bargaining rights in Wisconsin and Ohio, and attacks on the rights of women through state constitutional amendments.

The underlying assumptions of our Society and the American Dream must be fundamentally repaired before the genie of the Occupy Movement will go back in her bottle. Here are 10 ways the "Social Contract" is broken in the United States:

1. **Home Values.** Home ownership has long been the key to long-term prosperity for the American People. Homes paid for educations, retirements, and occasional vacations. Unfortunately, Wall Street was allowed to set aside regulations and add leverage upon leverage to the home mortgage market, which ultimately led to disaster. Now they are conspiring with real estate agents and appraisers to cram down home values, so that they can enjoy another 50-year run-up, primarily at the expense of the America People. This cycle of boom and bust cannot be allowed to continue, and there must be redress for the millions of homeowners damaged in the process. The American People were forced to save the too-big-to-fail financial institutions at the drop of a hat. Now it's the turn of the American People to be bailed out. We too cannot fail in this.

2. **Loans for Education.** A fundamental understanding of the American Dream has been that if we borrowed money to pay for college or community college

education, we could expect a reasonable job at the end of it, which would allow us to build a family and a comfortable life for the next generation and ourselves. Now America's youth is facing an economy that has been eaten out by the 1%. As one of the writers on the web site known as "WeArethe99Percent" aptly put it, "The best and brightest of my generation are bagging your groceries."

We used to talk about stakeholders in this country. It meant that each group had a stake in what went on in a corporation: shareholders; employees (both labor and management); and customers. No longer! The 1% has made it so even shareholders don't get a piece until they've taken their $100 million bonuses. I ask you, "Who is worth that much money?"

The youth of America is completely justified in demanding that the balance be restored before they are required to pay for their education loans.

3. Social Safety Nets in the Process of Destruction. The 1% is chiseling away at the social safety nets, which served and supported the American Dream for 75 years, since the Great Depression.

They are unwilling to pay their fair share for Social Security, putting the majority of the burden on average Americans, who earn significantly less than the $106,000 tax cap. This despite the fact that the 1% take the lion's share of the benefit out of our society in the form of things like roads for their trucks and education for their workers, which are paid for by all of us. When they pay their fair share, there is no problem with the financial health of Social Security.

They have been destroying Medicare from the inside out. They have been consistently attacking the family doctor, by reducing Medicare payments to the point where few doctors accept Medicare any longer. This year they propose to cut Medicare payments by 30%, which again forces the medical community to push back politically, rather than take care of America's health. If they succeed, we can say goodbye to healthcare with dignity in our old age.

They want to destroy Medicaid, rather than face the fact that most modern industrialized countries provide healthcare for their populations in a dignified manner. Americans do too, but it means that the more than 40 million Americans without health insurance cannot manage their routine healthcare needs. Instead, they must wait until there is a catastrophic illness. Then they go to the emergency room, and our system mysteriously takes care of the issue. Now the 1% wants to stop even that.

4. Labor Rights Are Being Destroyed. The American worker has spent a century fighting back the tycoons of the late nineteenth and early twentieth centuries, who wanted below minimum wage labor for their enterprises. Now we have to do it again! It is understandable that unions must bargain with management for their salaries and benefits. That's the nature of a capitalist society. But the attack on the collective bargaining rights of public employees and union members is outrageous. Luckily, this is the one over reach that has caused the American people to wake up and jump out of the pot. It is clear that the "Social Contract" will not be fixed until American conservatives stop their unjustifiable attack on collective bargaining rights.

5. Untrustworthy Banking System. The conservative mantra has been, "Freedom, freedom, give us freedom." Removing all the stops on the financial regulatory system invited the global financial meltdown, which has destroyed the value of our homes and the future of our children. No, the Occupy Movement will continue until the banking industry accepts sensible regulation once again, like the banking regulations, which made the second half of the twentieth century so prosperous.

6. Patriarchy Run Rampant. When women have their rights we will have peace in the world. The days of keeping the little woman barefoot and pregnant at home are over. While women get equal rights lip service in the United States, the reality is far different.

Conservative politicians keep throwing the "family values" hogwash in women's faces. All of them know that criminalizing abortion will save exactly zero babies, and yet they keep hyping the issue to distract the American people from what they are doing to our financial system. This is only one example of how the 1% keeps many women in line.

7. Defense Spending Out of Control. The 1% used the standard tactic of fear mongering to run up the defense budget, and take money from programs that supported the American dream. Wars created on the basis of lies were the justification for increasing defense spending by over $300 billion per year. But where is all of that money going? A ballistic missile submarine costs about $2 billion, but we haven't built more than a handful in the decade of the run-up, and very few surface ships. We've added about 27,500 men to the U.S. Marine Corps, but even granting that it costs $100,000 per year to field a Marine, that amounts to only a total additional cost of $2.75 billion per year. Comparable increases in manpower in the other services yield similar financial consequences. I say again, "Where is all of that money going?"

8. First Amendment Rights Threatened. The Right of Assembly and the Right to Petition the Government for a Redress of Grievances are two of the five fundamental rights found in the 1st Amendment of the Constitution of the United States. How is it that states and local governments have been allowed to establish laws abridging those rights? This has to change! If we don't demand the reinstatement of these Rights, we can look forward to losing the Rights of Freedom of Religion, Freedom of the Press, and Freedom of Speech in the future.

9. Retirement Threatened. By destroying the value of our homes and trying to break our contract for Social Security—yes, Social Security is a contract not an "entitlement" (which is a 1% buzz word suggesting it's a handout). If they are allowed to continue, none of us will have any savings, nor will we have the safety net of Social Security, which so many of us rely upon. How Americans afford to retire is fundamental to fixing the "Social Contract" in our country. The Occupy Movement will continue until this is properly addressed. And that means making the 1% pay their fair share in Social Security and Medicare taxes.

. Corrupt Attitude of Big Business. Over the past decade thousands of corrupt practices, many of them hugely costly to society, have crept into our society. Health insurance companies regularly deny legal and proper claims from doctors and hospitals over and over again. At the very minimum, they get to use the money owed to the doctors for a longer period, increasing their profits. Meanwhile, that creates additional administrative cost in our healthcare system.

Auto dealers pad repair bills with parts they didn't install. The banks take fees they don't deserve, and conspire with real estate agents and appraisers to drive down the value of our homes.

I could go on and on with this topic, but I don't need to, because everyone reading this knows what I mean. We have to demand higher standards of ethics from the business community and our politicians, or see our Society devolve to the corrupt practices standards of the developing world. As an American I expect and demand better!

Chapter 49: Social Contract v. Socialism

"The Best and Brightest of my generation are bagging your groceries. I am the 99%"

Conservative pundits, the mouthpieces for the 1%, try to throw the word "socialism" or "socialist" into everything they say about politics, particularly if they are criticizing President Obama or the Democratic Party. It's time to call them at their game, and show how they are using psychology to manipulate the American electorate.

Words are symbols, which have deep meaning in our subconscious minds. For those in my generation and older, "socialism" means the old Soviet Union, the "evil empire" that dominated Russian life for over 70 years. That was a system that famously did not work. So using the word in conservative rhetoric is a way of triggering our subconscious memories about something very evil and bad.

We must ask ourselves an important question. What was it about President Obama's message of "Change" that resonated so deeply with the American people? The answer is quite simply that the "Social Contract" is broken in our country, and we want it fixed!

Most of us have been feeling the pinch of the many ways the "Social Contract" is broken for decades, but finally the pain has reached a tipping point where the American people are ready to come out into the streets and proclaim that the status quo is unacceptable.

Many of us, me included, are disappointed with the first three years of the Obama Administration, because it has proven itself a toady of Wall Street instead of creating the change we sought. Any cursory glance at the situation that caused the global financial meltdown tells us that there was huge fraud and much felonious behavior going on across the full spectrum of the financial industry. And yet, disappointingly, except for hapless Bernie Madoff, no one has really been held responsible for that collapse. Instead, both the Bush and Obama Administrations threw a trillion dollars at the financial industry, and the "Masters of the Universe" went right on paying themselves $100 million bonuses for their brilliance in manipulating the rest of us. That needs to stop!

Americans have allowed ourselves to be distracted by endless debates about fraudulent family values like abortion, gay rights, and "intelligent design", while Wall Street has picked away at our children's future. I have been regularly reading a web site called "WeArethe99Percent", which perfectly sums up the fact that our "Social Contract" is broken in the United States. The quote, which appears at the beginning of this article, is an example, as is the following:

> "It is **unacceptable** that my situation is considered one of the "fortunate" ones and that I owe my life to what very little I do have. I want to work, and make an honest wage. I want to make a difference in my community and to my country. But every part of our financial system is preventing me from doing it. My peers are giving up their dreams in order to **survive** in this country.... This has to change.... We are the 99%."

What is the "Social Contract"? Since the time Jean-Jacques Rousseau explained the term, it amounts to our fundamental understanding about how society is supposed to work. People in each society intuitively accept different rules, but each society has its understandings among the people at large. As Rousseau put it, "Each of us places his person and authority under the supreme direction of the general will, and the group receives each individual as an indivisible part of the whole."

Americans have understood that fundamental to being American—our "Social Contract"--are the rights to live, be educated, have a job or build a business, raise a family, enjoy our retirement, and die with dignity. The Occupy Wall Street Movement reflects the fundamental fact that our "Social Contract" is broken. Each person coming to a rally may have a different point of pain, a different specific reason for coming into the streets, but we all feel in our bones that something is not right.

This is why the media has had such a difficult time of explaining what Occupy Wall Street is about. Each of our voices expresses a different point of pain, but the sum total of our voices is saying that the American "Social Contract" is broken. Something in our fundamental understandings about what it means to live in America and be an American has been taken away from us while we were distracted by "Dancing with the Stars", Major League Baseball, and a polarized politics that uses symbols like "socialism" rather than talking about our real issues.

There is a huge difference between the "Social Contract" and "Socialism". We want our Democracy back! We are the 99%!

Chapter 50: 55th Anniversary of Sputnik and How to Rebuild the Economy

October 4, 2012, 14:00 EDT. 55 years ago the Soviet Union launched Sputnik, the first Earth orbiting satellite. My father was a U.S. Naval officer at the time, and we were living near the major Navy base at Norfolk, Virginia. I don't really know how my parents were feeling when they heard the news, but I was worried. It didn't sound very encouraging considering our ongoing confrontation with the Soviets.

What followed were a series of failures of American rockets in test programs. These televised failures were equally disheartening, as was the launch of Soviet Cosmonaut Yuri Gagarin, the first human to orbit the Earth on April 12, 1961, just three months after the inauguration of President John F. Kennedy. Kennedy observed the importance of Sputnik in his "Special Message to Congress on Urgent National Needs" (May 25, 1961) as follows:

If we are to win the battle that is now going on around the world between freedom and tyranny, the dramatic achievements in space which occurrn recent weeks should have made clear to us all, as did the Sputnik in 1957, the impact of this adventure on the minds of men everywhere, whed io are attempting to make a determination of which road they should take.

He concluded with his immortal call to action:

I believe that this nation should commit itself to achieving the goal, before this decade is out, of landing a man on the Moon and returning him safely to Earth. No single space project in this period will be more impressive to mankind, or more important for the long-range exploration of space; and none will be so difficult or expensive to accomplish....

Kennedy had another part of his plan, though, and that was to re-energize the national economy, and it worked beautifully. By the height of the Apollo Program, 1966 (just 5 years later), 420,000 new jobs were created directly supporting the Space Program, and only 36,013 of them were in the government itself (*NASA Historical Data Book, 1958-1968*). The rest of them were in private industry, which created 1,200 new companies to support the program. Many other support jobs were created in restaurants, housing construction, butchers, bakers, and candle stick makers.

The benefit to the country cannot be overstated. The technological innovations, which stemmed from the Apollo Program, all of us benefit from today in the very computers by which you are reading this article. There were literally thousands of other benefits, from medicine and materials to jet fuels and many more support jobs, which were not included in NASA's figures above.

The total cost to the American taxpayer was miniscule, and was probably recovered by the income taxes on the hundreds of thousands of jobs that were created. Even in today's dollars, NASA is a huge bargain for the American people. The average cost of a Space Shuttle launch was only $1.5 billion over the entire 135 flights of the 30-year program. That's about $6.5 billion per year. That's 1% of our currently $650 billion defense budget.

We need to re-energize our economy, just as President Kennedy did. In the day, the usual suspects opposed him. In one of his typical prevarications, Mitt Romney said that creating a moon colony would cost "hundreds and hundreds of billions of dollars". His figures are simply untrue, and especially when you consider the recycling of tax dollars from the jobs that would be created by such a program, both in direct contractor jobs and service support jobs. I don't agree with Newt Gingrich much, but I do believe that committing the country to establishing a permanent moon colony, as mankind's next logical step into the Cosmos is highly appropriate, desperately needed by our economy, and an idea whose time has come. Our grandchildren will reap the benefits for decades, and thank us for making it possible.

Whoever the President is after January 20, 2017 should get on it without delay! There is no evidence that the Republicans would support such a program. They don't get it!

Chapter 51: We Saved Wall Street; Now Let's Save the Middle Class

Wall Street investment banks were allowed to create a giant casino over the past decade. They created a house of cards with risks at about 900:1. No wonder they were paying themselves $100 million bonuses. In Las Vegas, you can only get 35:1 odds on Roulette. When their house of cards collapsed, the life's savings of millions of Americans evaporated in a few months. Americans were called upon to "bail them out" with trillions of dollars, because they were "too big to fail." Now the Middle Class needs a bail out too!

Let us review the bidding:

1. Historically, banks were allowed to loan about 30 times more money than they actually had in their vaults. This is called leverage, and this is how they were able to make money. The system worked quite well over the second half of the Twentieth Century.

2. From June 16, 1933 to November 12, 1999, banks were regulated under Depression era bank reforms known as the Glass-Steagall Act (Banking Act of 1933). These chafed on bankers and Wall Street, but they fundamentally kept our economy safe from too much speculation.

3. After the Glass-Steagall Act was repealed in 1999, Wall Street was allowed to "syndicate" mortgages with essentially no regulation. Syndications were done in such an arcane way, that no government agency had a chance to understand what was going on in the market. What happened was Wall Street added an additional 30:1 leverage on top of the 30:1 leverage that already existed in the banks. This made the overall lever-

age on banking instruments something like 900:1 instead of 30:1 (30 x 30).

4. This was a great deal for Wall Street in the first decade of the 21st Century. They were giving mortgages away, because for every $1 banks loaned to consumers, Wall Street created a security "worth" $900. No wonder they were paying themselves $100 million bonuses.

5. Unfortunately, Wall Street created a lot of low quality mortgages; because the more they lent the more 900:1 benefit they received. The noise of Fannie Mae and Freddie Mac is Wall Street smoke and mirrors to hide the fact that Wall Street was many times worse. Indeed, those agencies were, in some small way, used to prove to the market that the junk securities Wall Street was creating were secure.

6. When Wall Street put the junk into too many syndicates, and a small percentage of the loans in those many syndicates failed, the house of cards came crashing down.

7. The crash that Wall Street created has destroyed and is continuing to destroy values in the real estate market. With 10-15 million homes in foreclosure or threat of foreclosure, the real estate market will not be able to clear the inventory for many years. The result is that there is no likelihood that real estate markets can recover for more than a decade. Officials are gradually starting to admit this.

8. Since the value of all outstanding residential mortgages owed by U.S. households to purchase residences housing four or fewer families was $9.9 Trillion as of year-end 2006, the loss to the Middle Class has been colossal compared to the Wall Street bailout. Our home is now appraised at 41.5% of its appraised value in 2004. If we extrapolate that loss in value across the residential housing market, that suggests that residential mortgages are now worth about $4.1 Trillion today, a loss of $5.8 Trillion. The losses to market values are even higher.

9. So, after Wall Street created the crisis through their casinos, and got bailed out, and the market has collapsed as a result, they are foreclosing on average Americans, who did nothing wrong, which is driving a reset of the entire economy and crushing the Middle Class, so they can just do it all again over the next 20-30 years.

10. This process needs to be stopped, and NOW! The 14.4% of mortgages that were delinquent or in foreclosure in September 2009, thanks to Wall Street

profligacy, are now pulling down the values of everyone's home, and crushing the retirement savings of a very large percentage of the Middle Class!

This situation is totally unfair, and Americans are looking to government to fix it! If you are wondering why people are in the streets demonstrating across the United States, and why the Occupy Movement will grow stronger in the coming year, this is one of the main reasons!

Culture Pot Full of Holes

Chapter 52: Culture Pot Full of Holes

Humpty Dumpty sat on a wall,
Humpty Dumpty had a great fall.
All the king's horses and all the king's men
Couldn't put Humpty together again.
Traditional English Nursery Rhyme

Culture takes a long time to develop—even millions of years. But Twitter™ and Facebook™ have shattered many cultures in less than a decade. This article is about the problem of evolving very quickly from the Analog Age to the Digital Age.

Dr. Carl G. Jung spoke about the development of language in *Psychology of the Unconscious*, first published as *Wandlungen und Symbole der Libido* in 1912. Dr. Jung explained that when two human beings wanted to communicate about a river there they must have used a sound, like "sshhhhhh" to identify the object of their discussion. He pointed out that the word "river" in nearly every language seems to include the sounds of running water. Later they developed other ways to differentiate which river from the trickle in a brook to the mighty Amazon.

Around each new designation a consensus developed among men and women about how to express the idea of river, and that was the beginning of culture. Soon after the earliest words, humans thought about the origin of these things in their world. After all, we are creatures who give meaning to what we see in our environment. But even that is exceedingly different.

Dr. Jung said that a word is like a wild animal, which we cannot control. When you see the word "river" for example, you have a specific idea of a river in your mind. I have no idea what that is, but I am satisfied that whatever image of a river exists in your mind, it will be close enough to my idea that you will follow my meaning. Even when we string a whole lot of these wild animals together, as I am doing in this essay, I can be fairly satisfied that you can get my meaning, though the animals are now roaming around in your unconscious, trying to find a way to get along with all of the others.

Culture is like that. As human groups, we have put in a lot of ingredients, no matter where we live in the world. Over time, we all have a general idea of how everyone else understands things in our environment, and we develop certain meaning that is common. As we do this, certain boundaries grow up among groups—perhaps not intentionally, but we have a tendency to think of our way and the other way.

I don't have to be very specific to make the point that the French, Italians, Spanish, Germans, and British all think of a variety of topics in very different ways. The same would be true of practically all national, religious, ethnic, and any other kind of group you might want to name. Most Americans will think about the song "America the Beautiful" in relatively the same way, even though we think about God in a completely different way.

These cultural groupings are very slow to change, but they do evolve over time, based on our experiences with other parts of the world. In my country, we have people from hundreds of differentiated groups, so we have inputs from many sources. Other countries may have been more like islands, where very little exposure to the outside world was present.

But now come along Twitter and Facebook, which can instantly connect everyone up to all of the inputs of humanity, both good and bad. Ideas, which challenge the *status quo*, can pass across boundaries and into thousands of minds in seconds rather than centuries. Last night I heard on television that one copy of *The Sunday New York Times* conveys more information than an Englishman of the 15th Century was exposed to in a lifetime. That Englishman had a long time to get used to new ideas.

Consider the plight of Galileo Galilei, who found things in his telescope that were different from the common understandings of his time. He wrote that he had learned that the Earth is not the Center of the Universe and God's creation. This was seen as a tremendous affront to the authority of The Roman Catholic Church, which said that it was. In fact, he was drawn up before The Inquisition and tried for heresy, at the age of 70.

Given his time, Galileo knew that he could not change the minds of a lot of thickheaded priests immediately, so he sent us a message that said he knew he was being treated unfairly by the rulers of his day. He knelt before the Inquisitors, put his hand on the Holy Gospels, and swore that the Earth was the Center of the Universe. He knew that the Church kept good records, and that his words would be kept forever. He made monkeys out of them!

He was never allowed to look through a telescope again, and he was held in a kind of house arrest, but he went on to develop two new sciences in the time he had left in his life. From June 22, 1633 , it took a very long time for the Pope to admit Galileo was right. Perhaps His Eminence has never admitted it, I don't know. But gradually, it became commonly accepted across the world that the Earth is not the Center of the Universe. That was the way cultures changed for millennia.

But now enter Twitter and Facebook, and the heresy is sloshing around the world, totally unstoppable, in seconds rather than decades or centuries. And it is not just on one fact, like the place of the Earth in the Universe. For some cultures those heresies are about almost everything that people have been taught since their childhood.

The pots that held a culture or a national way of doing things have suddenly been filled full of holes, they can't be fixed, and they don't hold water any longer. Depending on who you are, that is a big problem, and we are seeing that big problem play out on the world stage right now.

For me, I am all for the Rights of Freedom of Speech and Freedom of the Press, and all of the rest of the Rights most human beings hold dear, but all of us must be sensitive to the fact that it may take some of our brothers and sisters a little longer than others to make the change. Be a little sensitive with your tirades against what you perceive as backward ways. They have a lot of adjusting to do, and so do you! Some of those ways are time tested, and might be appropriate in your culture.

****

The Abjuration of Galileo Galilei

I, Galileo, son of the late Vincenzo Galilei, Florentine, aged seventy years, arraigned personally before this tribunal, and kneeling before you, Most Eminent and Reverend Lord Cardinals, Inquisitors-General against heretical depravity throughout the entire Christian commonwealth, having before my eyes and touching with my hands, the Holy Gospels, swear that I have always believed, do believe, and by God's help will in the future believe, all that is held, preached, and taught by the Holy Catholic and Apostolic Church. But whereas -- after an injunction had been judicially intimated to me by this Holy Office, to the effect that I must altogether abandon the false opinion that the sun is the center of the world and immovable, and that the earth is not the center of the world, and moves, and that I must not hold, defend, or teach in any way whatsoever, verbally or in writing, the said false doctrine, and after it had been notified to me that the said doctrine was contrary to Holy Scripture -- I wrote and printed a book in which I discuss this new doctrine already condemned, and adduce arguments of great cogency in its favor, without presenting any solution of these, and for this reason I have been pronounced by the Holy Office to be vehemently suspected of heresy, that is to say, of having held and believed that the Sun is the center of the world and immovable, and that the earth is not the center and moves:

Therefore, desiring to remove from the minds of your Eminences, and of all faithful Christians, this vehement suspicion, justly conceived against me, with sincere heart and unfeigned faith I abjure, curse, and detest the aforesaid errors and heresies, and generally every other error, heresy, and sect whatsoever contrary to the said Holy Church, and I swear that in the future I will never again say or assert, verbally or in writing, anything that might furnish occasion for a similar suspicion regarding me; but that should I know any heretic, or person suspected of heresy, I will denounce him to this Holy Office, or to the Inquisitor or Ordinary of the place where I may be. Further, I swear and promise to fulfill and observe in their integrity all penances that have been, or that shall be, imposed upon me by this Holy Office. And, in the event of my contravening, (which God forbid) any of these my promises and oaths, I submit myself to all the pains and penalties imposed and promulgated in the sacred can-

ons and other constitutions, general and particular, against such delinquents. So help me God, and these His Holy Gospels, which I touch with my hands.

I, the said Galileo Galilei, have abjured, sworn, promised, and bound myself as above; and in witness of the truth thereof I have with my own hand subscribed the present document of my abjuration, and recited it word for word at Rome, in the Convent of Minerva, this twenty-second day of June, 1633.

I, Galileo Galilei, have abjured as above with my own hand.

Chapter 53: Reflections on an Anniversary

It seems odd to be talking about the 10th "anniversary" of 9/11, because we have no real closure. Each of us harbors a queasy feeling at the base of our being that says the event is not over.

We know that despite the trillions of dollars that have gone into national defense, security systems, wars and reparations, on any given Sunday, not only Sunday, September 11, 2011, or on any day for that matter, something can happen that is even more horrific.

9/11 announced the existence of new global realities, which Americans had not noticed. But this changed world dropped into our living rooms on 9/11. The 10 years since have been our coping with the healing process. The fear mongers have used this opportunity to threaten our liberties in ways we do not even yet imagine.

But America was forged out of the chaos when "things were a mess." Every generation has faced its defining mess, and its own need for regeneration. The most obvious ones have been wars, but financial recessions and depressions have their own messy characteristics, as have the fights for rights by so many of our citizens. It is up to us to see our country through the mess. The instinct of many has been to grasp for fundamentalism, both religious and political, with the hope they could put things back the way they were. And they have been willing to give up a lot to do that. The reality is that the only way out is through, and we need to work as hard as our fathers and mothers to keep the essence of what has been earned with great sacrifice throughout the history of the United States.

There is a force at work in the world. Call it the urge to freedom for the human spirit. The United States of America has long been an embodiment of the success of that force, and most Americans have equally assumed that it was a done deal. We were wrong! We have been proud of our national accomplishments. We did not notice that most of mankind does not enjoy anything near our level of freedom. We thought of that as their problem.

At the same time, others have perceived that the United States has pursued international policies that have aided those who would prevent their countrymen from realizing the potential of that same human spirit of freedom. As such, the United States has been an impediment to those natural goals for many others in the world.

We need only refer to the "Arab Spring" to know that the human spirit is ultimately indomitable, and inconsistent American policies may cause us more harm than good in the perceptions and behaviors of the rest of the world.

It seems to me that what 9/11 tells us emphatically is that human kind must gradually fuse into one unity—perhaps not a perfect one, but one with respect for one another's differences. The American Founding Fathers knew that viscerally, adopting the Latin phrase "*E Pluribus Unum*" as our national motto. It means "From Many, One."

We have seen the power of that simple idea as it has evolved in North America over the past 400 years. A country filled with different perspectives of race, religion, political philosophy, financial skills, national origins and cultural backgrounds shows that we have the power to shape our own destiny. The United States has evolved because of the power of our Diversity--adopting good ideas from any group, while rejecting bad ideas that sometimes arise within every group.

Our result has brought prosperity to a vast number of Americans, while leaving much of the rest of the world living without electricity. We will need to change our perspective on mankind as a whole if our grandchildren will live in peace. 9/11 and the queasiness we still feel about what may come next proves that our destiny and the destiny of mankind are irrevocably linked. If there is a nod we must give to the day, let it be that it points to that inevitable link.

Chapter 54: We're Not Goint to Take Your guns; Enantiodromia Will

Enantiodromia (Greek: ἐνάντιος, enantios, opposite + δρόμος, dromos, running course) is a principle introduced by psychiatrist Carl Jung that the superabundance of any force inevitably produces its opposite. It is equivalent to the principle of equilibrium in the natural world, in that any extreme is opposed by the system in order to restore balance.

In the movie "Dangerous Liaisons," actor John Malkovich's character Valmont famously said, "It's beyond my control." So it is with the gun debate in the United States. The leadership of the National Rifle Association ("NRA") has convinced us consciously for years that their political power cannot be touched in the United States. They are wrong! When at least 26 innocents were killed in Newtown, Connecticut, all at one time, the psyche of the nation changed such that the NRA leaders will not have their way with us any longer.

Like wet sand at a beach, the shooting at Sandy Hook Elementary School caused the support to begin to recede beneath the seemingly impenetrable fortress of the NRA position. This will now continue at least until the United States reaches some sort of parity with the rest of world in terms of gun deaths. Neither I, nor anyone else who thinks we have too many guns at large in the United States, have to do anything to the "gun rights" found in the 2nd Amendment of the United States Constitution, such as they are.

The process already began some time ago. In the State of Maryland, for example, it is illegal to carry a handgun outside of a person's own property or their own place of business, except when transporting it from one to the other, or to an approved shooting range. The constitutionality of this statute is currently being challenged by Charles F. Williams, Jr., but the outcome of Mr. Williams' case is really irrelevant.

The case has already cost someone significant attorney's fees, and it is destined to cost much more as it moves to the United States Supreme Court, where the outcome is uncertain. Its irrelevance turns on the fact that, if it is ruled unconstitutional, Maryland can pass new statutes taking the ruling into consideration. The next attempt to attack the new statutes would again take several years and hundreds of thousands of dollars in legal fees, during which the new rules would be enforced.

Some years ago the streets of the City of New York were quite dangerous for casual pedestrians. It was commonplace to be "mugged", even in the vicinity of Broadway; not that it can't happen now, but much less frequently than before. Mayor Rudy Giuliani solved the problem by aggressively enforcing all of the small laws, like J-walking and littering. He also arrested scofflaws, who were jumping the subway turnstiles. When the arrests took place, he had the miscreants handcuffed together, and when the police department had a "full catch" of 10 or so, it marched them off to the police precinct for booking. It was amazing how many attorneys and accountants were arrested, but 20% of those arrested were found to have open warrants for their arrest pending. The white-collar people paid their bail and their fines, but those with outstanding warrants found themselves in jail and in trials for their bigger crimes, including back child support.

What will happen across the United States is much like the New York experience. First, states and municipalities can, and in many cases do, require registration of firearms. To the extent that gun shows and long guns are exempt from such registrations, those statutes can be changed. Then, if the police arrest someone for something as simple as a minor traffic violation, they can perform a search if they have reason to believe there are weapons in the vehicle. Finding an unregistered weapon, they can confiscate and destroy it, and enforce the penalties for possessing an unregistered weapon. It seems to me very unlikely that registration statutes do conflict with the 2nd Amendment to the Constitution of the United States.

But more daunting to current gun owners will be the good works that can be enforced by Wall Street, in ways that have nothing to do with the 2nd Amendment. **Insurance companies can and should include provisions in their homeowners and personal liability policies, which require that all weapons in a household be properly registered with local authorities and kept secure under lock and key.**

If something then happens with a weapon registered to you, you can be held personally liable by any victim; your homeowner's insurance can be voided; and criminal penalties may apply. Personal liability should include your personal estate, whether or not you die in the illegal event, as was the case of Nancy Lanza, the mother of the Newtown shooter.

This would mean that if you die while owning a legally registered weapon, and that weapon is later used in a crime, your personal estate could be touched by the victims, if it has not already been dispersed. Indeed, if I were counsel to any of the Newtown victims, I would include such an action in my legal proceedings in any case.

Nancy Lanza could possibly be found negligent for not properly controlling her weapons, particularly in the face of knowing the mental condition of her son. I would immediately move the Surrogate Court for a temporary restraining order denying the settlement of her estate until the matter could be properly adjudicated.

All of my gun-owning friends claim that they are responsible adults, who are properly trained to handle their firearms. I am sure they are correct. In fact, I am satisfied that at least 99.9% of all gun owners deal with their firearms properly. As a result, they would have nothing to worry about if their insurance policies contained such provisions.

Life insurance policies currently exclude payment on suicide only for the first two years after issuance. They can and **should be changed such that if someone is found to have committed suicide with a firearm, the policy will not be paid.** Indeed, they should exclude all suicides in any case.

Statutes can be passed requiring the registered gun owner to pay any and all costs incurred by a governmental entity, including school districts, in the event a firearm registered to them is used in an unlawful act.

Why do my friends, who love to brandish their guns, now feel the need to post photographs of themselves with their beloved weapons? Because, in their subconscious, they know that these and other measures to restrict accessibility to firearms are coming.

Many of my friends are military veterans, who know very well that weapons are not just strewn around aboard ships and on bases. Rather, military firearms are maintained in armories, under lock and key—a custom that dates back several hundred years. Why should the maintenance of civilian weapons be less careful than military weapons? There are reasons the United States Armed Forces have such policies. They are known to reduce accidental gun deaths among military personnel.

Public opinion has bubbled to the surface, aided by the NRA and my friends, who want people to see them with their weapons. Suggestions to arm teachers in schools, or send in vigilante Dads, who love their guns, will only reinforce their opposition. It is one thing to have armed and trained police officers in schools, but that isn't how it will play out. If some municipalities do such a thing, in sufficient number to make a difference, they will soon find the costs prohibitive. Remember, there was an armed Deputy Sheriff on the campus of Columbine High School on April 20, 1999, the day of the massacre. Who wants an alcoholic or drug abusing volunteer Dad watching over their children with semi-automatic weapons?

In summary, the process is on, and times are changing. The principle of *Enantiodromia* is already operational in the psyches of Americans. Politicians supported by the NRA will start to lose elections; insurance companies and courts will start making gun ownership more costly, something that cannot be stopped by the 2nd Amendment; and rational and responsible gun owners will act even more responsibly than they have been already.

I predict we will see a vast decrease in the number of gun deaths in the United States, and that won't be attributable to the behavior of the NRA, which is a lobbyist for the gun industry. As has become abundantly clear by the ridiculous prescription proposed by this lobby, which benefits from the selling of more and more guns, they have very little real concern for the safety of our population at large.

P.S. It is interesting to note that the story of American Hero Wyatt Earp is in part a story about gun control. The shootout at the O.K. Corral was all about disarming the "Cowboys". It's also interesting that Wyatt Earp did believe in abiding by gun control laws personally. He checked his revolver at the U.S. Marshall's office in Juneau, Alaska on June 27, 1900, as was required by local ordinance, but never picked it up. His steamer departed at 5:00 a.m. on the 29th, before the Marshall's Office opened.

Mythologizing

Chapter 55: MH370 and the Importance of Answers

The disappearance of Malaysian Airlines Flight No. 370 last month gives us a very clear example of how the news has died, and how media tycoons like Rupert Murdoch can control major voting blocks of the global electorate. Human beings cannot stand uncertainty. We need there to be an explanation for everything in our world, no matter how specious, or we feel uneasy.

Why have CNN, Fox News and other "news" reporting organizations devoted so much time and money to the reporting of the MH370 story? Why has Mary Schiavo, former Inspector General of the Department of Transportation become an international celebrity? The answers to these questions are very simple. Several "news" stories have reported that the viewership of most major "news" outlets has increased substantially because of the mystery. Media organizations, peopled by no fools, at least almost none, give us "news" stories that bring eyeballs to their advertisers, whether or not they provide new information and regardless of other important news in the world.

Why are we humans so interested in the MH370 mystery? A very large percentage of the population of the world with access to television fly somewhere regularly. Without an explanation for the mystery of MH370, we naturally feel anxiety about what it means for our own lives. If we are honest with ourselves, very few of us really care about the lives of those lost.

The mystery happened to people few of us would ever meet in a lifetime, in an area of the world that is far far away from everything we know. Many more important stories have been hidden from view, until they were too hot to avoid, and even now they take second billing behind MH370.

Though the Russian takeover of Crimea can be regarded as an event leading to a new Cold War, few of us even knew anything of significance was taking place in Ukraine for the months leading up to Russia's seizure. The media had us more interested in whether Shaun White would win another Gold Medal in the Olympics in Sochi than whether a new threat was emerging to our national well being.

The human mind cannot accept uncertainty. From the time we are born, we have to find the answers. As a newborn, one of the first things we notice is that we are hungry. We don't know much, but we must find the answer to the question of how we will solve that existential problem. Fortunately, a benevolent goddess, our Mother, supplies the answer from the cacophony of things that are happening to us after the trauma of birth. As a result, we become bonded to her for life.

After we've answered that question, we go on answering questions about our existence for the rest of our lives. The MH370 mystery is no different. If we often fly in airplanes, we cannot feel comfortable until we know what threat it represents, and can evaluate the danger to ourselves. Without an explanation for the disappearance of a very large airplane, many of us will feel major anxiety the next time we board an airplane.

Think of all of the explanations our controllers in the media have offered to us in the last month. They have our minds spinning with uncertainty. The pilots were overcome by a terrorist or an explosion in the equipment; the pilots had criminal intent themselves; a third party called the airline and threatened to detonate a nuclear, biological, or chemical weapon onboard if the pilot did not fly to a remote location somewhere in the world, where the passengers are being held hostage; space aliens abducted the plane; and many more. I expect the "History" Channel to start airing the space alien theory on incessant documentaries at any moment.

Yes, gradually the story will start to recede from the headlines, but this MH370 mystery will have interminable pulling power for the media until it is fully explained. They can trot out a "new theory" any time they want to divert our attention from something that is actually of real importance to us, like what is happening in Syria. Ah, did you forget that the bipolar halves of the Muslim world are tearing each other apart, and the outcome will have significant impact on our personal fortunes and the health of our sons and daughters for the rest of their lives? Where is the reporting on that?! It's times like these when I feel like a steer with a ring through my nose, and I'm being led to the slaughter by the benevolent men who have been feeding me from their Wall Street penthouses. I know it, but can do nothing about it. I'm trapped in a herd that doesn't even know where we're going, nor do they really care. What to do?!

No worries! The Army-Navy Game is on, and then I'm going to Home Depot and Giant to pick up a chain saw and a lemon. [That's called avoidant coping.] Let the kids and grand babies worry about their own future!

Metaphor Credit: I acknowledge the brilliance of Professor Sheldon Solomon of the Psychology Department of Skidmore College for the "chain saw and a lemon" metaphor. Dr. Solomon is a leader in The Ernest Becker Foundation and one of the early proponents of "Terror Management Theory." He taught me about avoidant coping during an interview we had in 2005.

Chapter 56: American Exceptionalism

"Can you say why America is the greatest country in the world?"

Coming from her own subconscious doubt and insecurity about the answer, a college sophomore asked that question in the opening scenes of HBO's "The Newsroom." Why is it that we always need to be reassured about this question? Could it be that deep inside we have a queasy feeling that it is no longer true?

Newsroom anchor Will McAvoy (Jeff Daniels) delivers one of the most articulate rebuttals to the idea that America is the greatest straight from the pen of Emmy Award winning Writer and Producer Aaron Sorkin.

This video can be found on Youtube as "The Newsroom 2012 Opening Scene"

Olympics 2012 gives us a useful opportunity to examine greatness in context. After the 1924 Paris Olympics and the 1981 movie Chariots of Fire, the conventional wisdom of the day was that Harold Abrahams, winner of the 1924 100 Meter dash, was the "fastest man in the world." Was he? That's highly doubtful, considering the fact that only 44 countries participated in the 1924 games, and only two from Africa, Egypt and South Africa. Neither the newly established Soviet Union nor China was represented. Even Germany, which was still struggling with the aftermath of World War I, was not present. Abrahams' time of 10.6 seconds has now been eclipsed by the current world record of 9.58 seconds.

If the London 2012 Olympic Games tell us anything, it is that all human beings everywhere in the world are really just about the same. Though the commentators ballyhoo the medalists, the truth is that the winners differ from the losers by only 100ths of a second or scoring point. Even in the very long cycling road races, which for men was 152.5 miles and for women 78.5 miles, the difference from the 1st to the 40th finishers was less than one minute, and the difference between a gold and silver medal was a single bike length or less.

Am I implying that the United States of America is not the greatest country in the world? Since I'm an American, I am obliged to say that it is; but I have my reasons too. Greatness does not come from the measures described by Will McAvoy in "The Newsroom," but rather from the fact that despite all of our differences, and this year those seem particularly deep, the dynamism of a country built by the sons and daughters of every nation, race, culture and religion on Earth continues to be unmatched. Our Diversity is our gift from God.

This year Republican politicians want to sell us fear of Iran and China as a first priority, but those countries are no match for the United States on any measure. Iran can rattle its sabers all it wants, but it cannot change the fact that the United States spends 100 times as much on our armed forces as Iran. Should we be afraid of Iran's "nuclear threat"? Well, maybe a little, but Iranians should be far more afraid of it. Why? Because, if some Iranian official foolishly does attack the United States or one of our allies with even one weapon, the Iranian government would be ended forthwith. What sensible person in the world would doubt that?

In the case of China, the United States imported nearly $400 Billion of products from China during 2011. If that business were suddenly to evaporate, as it surely would in the event of a serious military confrontation with China, China would suffer huge domestic unemployment, and would find itself fighting its own population. In such case, many WalMart and Sam's Club customers would be upset because of an increase in prices, but not more. The China example demonstrates the strength and importance of the American economy, which Will McAvoy didn't mention in his soliloquy, but which is highly relevant.

Still, the Olympics show us once again that we in the United States cannot be complacent about anything. The Chinese and Japanese athletes, who were no physical match for Americans in the first half of the 20th Century, have now had plenty of protein for decades, and their athletes are beating Americans left, right and center.

In many ways, Michael Phelps provides us with an apt metaphor for the United States itself. Like Phelps after the 2008 Olympics, the United States was the world's dominant country after World War II, and particularly after the end of the "Cold War". But our edge has slipped a bit, thanks to too many factors to name. Proteins, Facebook, and Twitter are just three that easily come to mind for anyone who can read this and use their brain.

What the last five decades has shown us clearly is that all human beings live on one very fragile planet, at least 350,000 years travel time from the nearest place that could provide a valid alternative for life once our Sun and the Earth no longer support our needs properly. On our planet, the next few decades are going to see serious dislocations, which will make the trials of the 20th Century seem like kindergarten.

The Chinese are damming the headwaters of the Ganges River, which provides water to half a billion people in India. Meanwhile, global warming is melting the Himalayan glaciers to such a degree that the Chinese dams may find themselves high and dry. India and China both must build the equivalent of one coal powered electrical power plant every week for the rest of the 21st Century, just to keep up with their population growth, and the demands can become hugely more complex in later centuries. Without water, growing food will become a major problem and lead to devastating shortages beyond the power of any government to help, regardless of how well meaning it is.

The Indian, Chinese, and Iranian examples are only a few of the issues that will face our grandchildren. There are similar dislocations in the offing everywhere. One only need go to the movies or turn on the TV to see how we are subconsciously preparing ourselves for a worse case scenario. "Hunger Games" and "Revolution" come immediately to mind.

The Olympics are great. They show us competition is good. For every young person we see at the games, it is very likely that 100 or 1,000 also competed back home, and made themselves and their future generation stronger. But one thing is clear, and that is that we must outgrow the idea that one country can dominate all of the others. Given the advantages we have had in the 20th Century in the United States, even through some very rough times, others will excel, and they will have their own ideas of how our problems will be solved going forward.

These are some of the reasons why the fictional sophomore revealed her subconscious queasiness about American greatness in the first episode of "The Newsroom." The reason is that by many measures the United States is no longer "the greatest country in the world," and that isn't even the issue anymore anyway.

It is time for us to outgrow our myopic perspective, and realize that everyone in the world is going to have to find better ways to cooperate. The Olympic Games offer us a great metaphor for how that can be done. We just need to see our world leaders paying attention and actually leading, rather than always wanting to go to guns and set us back several centuries. These days that strategy just leads to a circular firing squad.

Chapter 57: Alexander Hamilton: American Hero

"The sacred rights of mankind are not to be rummaged for among old parchments or musty records. They are written, as with a sunbeam, in the whole volume of human nature, by the hand of the divinity itself; and can never be erased or obscured by mortal power."

It is easy to point to many heroes of the American experience, but few can claim the stature of Alexander Hamilton. He was a revolutionary before he was 21, and a hero of sufficient note that George Washington named him his Aide-de-Camp at age 21, and later his Chief of Staff.

On the morning after Washington's "Crossing of the Delaware," on December 26, 1776, Hamilton's artillery proved decisive in stopping Hessian troops during the Battle of Trenton. He lined up the artillery pieces he had recently liberated from the British at The Battery, in lower Manhattan, and aimed them down a major Trenton thoroughfare. When the Hessians moved to assemble to fight off Washington's assault, Hamilton's weapons decimated their ranks.

George Washington came to know of Hamilton's deeds, and invited him to join his Headquarters. During the winter in Valley Forge, 1777-78, Washington had no communication with his northern army, under General Gates. He assigned the then 23-year-old Lieutenant Colonel the task of riding four days through the snow to Albany, to consult with General Gates about his plans for the spring campaign of 1778.

Washington told Hamilton, "Tell Gates to come down in the spring and take up my left flank, along the Hudson. But," he said, "listen to General Gates's plan, and if his plan is better than mine, tell him to follow his own plan." Thusly, the young Alexander Hamilton was given the responsibility for deciding the deployment of the Continental Army for the 1778 campaign.

Always anxious for a command of his own, Hamilton was finally given command of a New York light infantry battalion before the Battle of York-town, in 1781. In the final assault at Yorktown, Hamilton commanded three battalions, and took Redoubt #10 with bayonets. This action effectively ended the operations of British troops in the American colonies.

Alexander Hamilton's influence on our American form of government is still felt today. He is credited with publishing 51 of the 85 essays, now known as The Federalist Papers. The other authors were James Madison (29 essays) and John Jay (5 essays).

These papers are still among the primary citations in matters of constitutional law, which is the purview of the Supreme Court of the United States. Hamilton always enjoyed the confidence of George Washington, who named him our first Secretary of the Treasury, serving side by side with Secretary of State Thomas Jefferson. Though it may seem strange in these contentious times, his support of the creation of a "national debt" was the one factor above all others, which assured the strength of the United States to this day. In 1790, the northern states were still struggling with debts they had undertaken in order to fight the Revolutionary War. Most of the southern states had handled their debts quickly. The economic situation of the day was that northern states maintained very small farms, like that of our 2nd President, John Adams, which paled next to the plantations of hundreds of acres operated by slave owners like our 3rd President, Thomas Jefferson. Because of his responsibility as Secretary of Treasury, Hamilton understood that something needed to give the federal government authority to collect revenues, in order to build up its stature, as compared to that of individual states, and thereby bind it together as one entity.

In June 1790, Jefferson ran into a haggard Hamilton outside the office of President George Washington in New York. Hamilton had lost arguments with Congress to establish a "national debt" over the preceding two months. Jefferson wanted something too. Sixteen sites had been proposed for the Capital of the United States, but Jefferson and his fellow Virginians wanted it to be in Virginia.

There was a fear at the time that the new country could revert to a situation of separate countries, something like Europe. Hamilton understood this risk, and the fact that the country would be much weaker if it did not "hang together."

Jefferson offered to organize what has become known as "The Dinner Party," on June 20, 1790. Present were James Madison, representing the southern states, Hamilton, representing the northern states, and Thomas Jefferson as host. In that evening, the three men agreed that the Nation's Capital would be in Virginia (later changed to the District of Columbia, taken from Virginia and Maryland), and that the Federal Government would assume the Revolutionary War debts of the northern states.

Afterward, the three men made it so with their political allies, thus creating the "national debt" of the United States of America, and thereby giving the country its first credibility in the world of finance. In these contentious times regarding our "national debt" it is important to note that from that time to this, the United States of America has never failed to honor its debts. This has proven to be one of the great strengths of the United States in world affairs.

While Secretary of the Treasury, Hamilton was instrumental in creating the Cutter Service, which was a precursor of the United States Coast Guard. When relations with France soured during the Presidency of John Adams, Hamilton was appointed a Major General, and became the second officer to hold the rank of Senior Officer of the U.S. Army, after George Washington himself, who was a generation older. Among his many contributions to the Army was his advocacy of establishing the U.S. Military Academy at West Point.

Like most heroes, Alexander Hamilton had his flaws, but few can deny that he is one hero who was on the leading edge of the American fight for freedom of the human spirit, and one of the chief architects of the success of the United States of America as an independent nation.

Sweet Land of Liberty

Chapter 58: You Live in a Free Country

Congress shall make no law respecting an establishment of religion, or prohibiting the free exercise thereof; or abridging the freedom of speech, or of the press; or the right of the people peaceably to assemble, and to petition the Government for a redress of grievances.[1] The 1st Amendment to The Constitution of the United States, Proposed to the States September 25, 1789; adopted December 15, 1791.

This article is about our Rights and Freedoms, and how difficult they are to win and maintain in the 21st Century, nearly 400 years after my first ancestors came to North America.

"You live in a free country" are nearly the first words I can remember my Father saying to me. I don't remember why, but I found the assertion very comforting at the time. I must have been about ten years old. Two years later my Grandfather took me and my then 10-year-old brother to Manhattan for the first time. At The Battery, while waiting for the ferry to Liberty Island, he told us the story of our first ancestor in North America, Wolfert Gerritsen Van Couwenhoven, who left Holland in 1625 and became one of the first 200 European settlers of Manhattan Island, along with his wife and three sons.

They were refugees from the 80 Years' War, when the Spanish Catholics were coming to Holland every summer to beat the Reformed Dutch back into the Catholic Church. They just wanted to live their lives in peace and Freedom. It seems silly to us today, but that is the way things were back then. Their story of Freedom is more fully told in *The Island at the Center of the World: The Epic Story of Dutch Manhattan and the Forgotten Colony That Shaped America*, by Russell Shorto.

As long as there was plenty of land in the world, it was always possible to move away from the existing oligarchy of the day, and build a new life far from civilization. My ancestors before Wolfert were likely people like that. They moved into the "low countries," which the oligarchy of their day probably viewed as a swamp. Dutchmen have a joke, which you can hear on sightseeing cruises around Amsterdam to this day, which says, "God made heaven and earth, but we Dutch built Holland ourselves." Wolfert followed their example, and voted with his feet, by moving to the New World. That time for the human species of the 21st Century is long since past.

It is important to note the often-made comment that Rights are never given. They are taken. They must be taken from people who would cram down our throats their views about how to live our private lives. We see that playing out on our television screens and on Internet postings this very day. People around the world are taking their Rights from those who would deny them. This is never easy, and it does take time.

Even the American 1st Amendment, which I consider the bedrock of our American society, was not easy, and it is still in flux. The American Revolution officially began with a Declaration of Independence, which was proclaimed in Philadelphia 237 years ago today. But it had been in the works for at least 130 years before that. My ancestors sought their Freedom of the New Amsterdam Colony from Holland in the 1640s, and Benjamin Franklin was talking about a separate country in the 1750s. He worked on the project for the rest of his life.

But from July 4, 1776, it took over 15 years to even agree on the terms of the 1st Amendment. We have been interpreting it ever since. The original Articles of Confederation and Perpetual Union of The United States of America was agreed on November 15, 1777, but it was a flawed document. It was the basis of our existence as a nation, but it took until March 4, 1789 before The Constitution of the United States could be agreed by 9 of the original 13 colonies.

The Constitution is the basis of our strong country today, because it balances power among three equal branches of government. The Executive (President) enforces the laws that are passed by the Legislature (Congress—House and Senate), which are interpreted as to whether they are in the spirit of the original intent of the Founders of our country by the Judiciary (Supreme Court of the United States).

But the Constitution could not contain the Rights of the 1st Amendment, because the Founders could not get everyone to agree on just what Rights we should have. That could only happen with the passage of the 1st 10 Amendments to the Constitution, which are our "Bill of Rights". These were ratified by three-fourths of the States on December 15, 1791.

Since then, The Supreme Court of the United States has been interpreting our Rights, and we have all agreed to abide by their decisions, whether we agree or disagree. The balance comes because if we disagree, we can go back to the legislature and try again. It is a messy process, but over the course of our history, we have built a strong and powerful nation, of which we are justifiably proud.

There is little wonder that we are seeing people around the world struggle with why it takes so long to change things today. Changes take time and persistence. Sometimes we get it wrong in the process, and people come into the streets in disgust, but that is the beauty of our 1st Amendment, which allows us to peaceably assemble and seek a redress of our grievances. It can be argued that some in governments at many levels in the United States have forgotten these Rights, but that is the subject for another article.

Chapter 59: Sweet Land of Liberty

The 4th of July, 2011 was a most memorable one for me. My wife and I had the honor of attending the Citizenship Ceremony for new Americans at the William Paca [pronounced PayKa] House & Gardens in Annapolis, Maryland. What struck me most about the event was that these 38 new Americans understand better than many native born Americans what being an American really means. Each of them left a life, a family, and a cultural heritage to join us in "the land of the free and the home of the brave."

For we Americans, there is nothing very unusual about that. Every human being in North America is either an immigrant, or descended directly from someone who was. This is true of even so-called "native Americans," since there were no human beings at all in North or South America before 13,000 years ago, a virtual blink in human existence.

I often ask my fellow Americans what one factor above all others is the reason for the strength and success of the United States of America. Few have a clear-cut answer. I believe our strength is our Diversity, which I see as the Glory of God.

Unlike monolithic societies, where one person or group dominates everyone in various nefarious ways, in the United States we have hundreds of groups of very different national origin, religions, races, and points of view. Whenever one of these groups has a good idea, everyone adopts it. I use Starbucks as my example of a good idea, which is now adopted globally. Whenever a bad idea emerges, the other groups pound it out of the system by vigorous debate. It is a tempering process, like that used in making steel. Slavery is my example of a bad idea.

The day was made more special for me by sharing it with our guest, Lama Phurbu Tashi Rinpoche, a Tibetan Buddhist monk and a refugee, who plans to be another new American in a couple of years. Watching him interact with the period costumed actors representing the 1st Maryland Regiment and the Colonial Ladies was a particular treat.

Because of his saffron and purple robes, many at the event, including the news media, thought he was one of the day's honorees, so he was interviewed several times.

The Director of the Baltimore office of the Immigration Service told us that they create new citizens every day—18,000 or so in Maryland each year. But this event on the 4th of July is a particularly meaningful occasion. The venue in the William Paca House & Gardens is within a block of the 1st Capitol building of the United States, the Maryland State House.

William Paca was one of 4 signers of the Declaration of Independence from Maryland. Whenever I give visitors tours of Annapolis, I always point out the magnificent mansions of these courageous men, to show what they were putting at risk when they signed the document. They were committing treason against the British Crown, and, as Benjamin Franklin put it succinctly, "We either hang together or we will hang separately!" After the ceremony, I mentioned to one of the new Americans that, as an American, I am very proud of them, because they know the meaning of being an American better than many of our native born countrymen. I told one, "You know what it means to be an American, so if we forget, you remind us!"

Lama Phurbu Tashi Rinpoche became an American Citizen on April 10, 2014.

CONCLUSION

"There ain't no answer.
There ain't gonna be any answer.
There never has been an answer.
That's the answer."
Gertrude Stein

The issues we face in politics today have been with us for a long time, and many of them are full of irony. Gertrude Stein and Claribel and Etta Cone were lesbians at the turn of the 20th Century. They lived quite unconventional lives for the time, and even today they would likely struggle. All three women collected art, much of which defined Modern Art as we know it today.

If it weren't for these three avid art collectors, we might not know so much of Pablo Picasso, Vincent Van Gogh, Paul Gauguin, Pierre-Auguste Renoir and Henri Matisse. They were part of the Paris arts community of the early 20th Century that included in their circle Ernest Hemingway, F. Scott Fitzgerald, Sinclair Lewis, Ezra Pound, and Thornton Wilder among many others. They sponsored these artists when they were still in the "starving artist" category, or in the case of Van Gogh, already forgotten.

Stein's salons of the day amounted to a hot house where the cross fertilization of ideas that drove western society in the 20th Century could take place. Their collections are legendary, and the Cone Collection at the Baltimore Museum of Art is now valued in excess of $1 billion. Their influence on modern society is really beyond estimation.

Even today the Cone Sisters' sexual orientation is obfuscated in their Wikipedia entries. The irony is that they were instrumental in birthing the

Modern Art that is today beloved on a worldwide basis, and is in the bedrock of our culture. Go to any major city in the world and you are likely to find a major exhibition of the art of these luminaries to this very day.

There are few, even among the most conservative of fundamentalist Christians, who don't appreciate some or all of the contributions from this group of intellectuals, and yet it was Stein and the Cone Sisters, who were largely responsible for giving them their start when times were tough.

My point is that practically no one would say anything other than that society was hugely benefitted by their lives, and an argument could be made that their sexual orientation may have played a significant part in that contribution. One story has it that Stein and Claribel Cone were lovers during their time together at the Women's Medical College of Johns Hopkins University. As a result of their long-term friendship, the Cone sisters often visited Stein in Paris, and were introduced to the artistic luminaries of the day.

On a different topic, television's #1 most popular show, *The Last Ship*, is indicative of that fact that we are projecting our collective anxiety about the possibility of a biological attack on our public health. This is exacerbated by the recent Ebola epidemic, which the World Health Organization has now raised to its highest level of warning.

It has happened before, and one of the ironies here is that if it had not been for the Influenza Pandemic of 1918, you would not be reading this right now. You see my grandfather was engaged to a woman, who was not my grandmother. On one weekend in August of 1918, she and her 4 sisters died of the flu on one weekend. As a result, my broken hearted grandfather later married my grandmother, and so I can write this now.

This begs the question of what will all of the Christian fundamentalists do if a true epidemic arrives in the United States again? I mean the ones who refuse to have their children immunized. Will they be desperately demanding immunization like the rest of us? Why are they not getting their children immunized against flu every year?

Approximately 675,000 American died of flu in 1918-19, and 20-40 million died worldwide. That's more than died in all of World War I, and the Black Death Bubonic Plague of 1347-51. Why are some politicians pushing scientific ignorance? Don't they realize it will be their ignorant constituents, the people who elect them, who would be most likely to die?

Then there is the issue of abortion, which conservatives continue to promote. My grandmothers had 5 abortions between them in the 1920s, a fact my mother felt important enough to tell me on her deathbed. Why? Because those were two conservative women, daughters of the Victorian Age, who would never dream of committing a crime. And yet they committed 5 felonies between them, and supported the shadow economy of felonious medical doctors, who were assisting such women.

Why would we ever want to return our society to those horrific days? Today, even if we banned abortion in the United States, women of means would inexpensively go to Canada or Europe for their procedures, and poor women will continue to do what they've always done. If they have their babies, society will refuse to help support them or will incarcerate them, at a cost of at least $35,000 per year. Why not just raise the minimum wage and pay them that much? Is it because it's more profitable to run a prison than pay a living wage? What, pray tell, are we thinking? Banning abortion will save no babies, but this is a favorite hobbyhorse of those who want to offer smoke and mirrors for solutions to our problems rather than real solutions.

Drs. James Hillman and Sonu Shamdasani, in their conversations about Dr. Carl Jung's The Red Book, collected in a recent book called *Lament of the Dead*, talked about how we are lived by our dead. We see this on our television screens every night, with racial conflicts still going on in the United States nearly five decades after the murders of Dr. Martin Luther King, Jr. and Robert F. Kennedy, and religious conflicts across the globe, which had their origins in Jerusalem more than two thousand years ago.

When will humanity wake up?! The venal men who use our dead and our prejudices to manipulate our minds and control our futures can only be stopped if humanity wakes up to what they are doing. The talking heads on cable television only pour gasoline on these centuries old conflicts and attitudes as a means to manipulate us. Only when a few of us gain enough influence to wake up everyone else will this have any chance of changing.

Some places around the world are more enlightened than others. Yes, it is true. But the Internet and social networking have become great equalizers, and developments that took centuries in Western Europe, can be accomplished in years or decades in other parts of the world. They no longer have to be settled with wars and murder.

Women. who were isolated in their societies, without having interaction with other women from around the world, can now communicate with women of all faiths and ethnic groups. They can see what's right and what's wrong in how they're treated. Change can only come when the problems are understood! Change is coming to the world, ready or not!

I certainly empathize with the woman photographed in a recent women's rights rally, who carried a sign saying: "I can't believe I still have to protest this shit!" I understand that she feels these issues were settled in the late 1960s and early 1970s in the United States, so why should we be arguing about them now? The answer is that we must fight for our rights in every generation. Liberty is never finally won!

Venal politicians will try to exploit every weakness they see in society to manipulate us in a way that allows them to control our futures against our individual best interests. In other countries they do this with guns and tear gas. Here tear gas is coming into a new vogue, but mostly they do it with endless television harangues. We must be constantly vigilant and awake, and we must remember Yogi Berra's dictum:

"It's only over when it's over."

ACKNOWLEDGEMENTS

I am most grateful for the creative work that went into the production of Political Psychology.

Me Design researched and created the concept, performed the layout design, cover design and worked with me on the concepts for the book's visuals. *www.me-design.me*

Rebecca Sutherland is the illustrator, who helped develop our concepts and produce the shadow puppets, which are such an integral part of the message of this book. *rebeccasutherland.co.uk*

Laura Lewis photographed the shadow puppets at her London studio, Double L Studios, creating brilliant images that really brought the puppets to life. *www.lauralewisphotography.co.uk*

Dr. Jean Raffa wrote the gracious Foreword. She is an author, speaker, and leader of workshops, dream groups, and study groups. She maintains a blog called Matrignosis: A Blog About Inner Wisdom. Her job history includes teacher, television producer, college professor, and instructor at the Disney Institute in Orlando and The Jung Center in Winter Park, FL. She is the author of three books, a workbook, a chapter in a college text, numerous articles in professional journals, and a series of meditations and short stories for Augsburg Fortress Publisher.

Her most recent book is Healing the Sacred Divide. Her The Bridge to Wholeness: A Feminine Alternative to the Hero Myth (LuraMedia, 1992) was nominated for the Benjamin Franklin Award for best psychology book of 1992. Reviewed in several journals and featured on the reading lists of university courses, it was also picked by the Isabella catalogue as a must-read for seeking women.

IMAGE DISAMBIGUATION

Images always mean different things to each individual, and some of those meanings cannot even be known, because they exist in our subconscious mind. Part of what any writer does is to draw a picture in the psyche of the reader. Each of us imagines the characters of a nobel, as well as its settings and action, but because we all come to a novel with different experiences, those images will be slightly different.

The images in Political Psychology are intentionally simple and ambiguous, in order to give the reader the most psychic field in which to consider their implications. Each one intentionally has at least three levels of meaning: psychological; symbolic; and political, but no doubt each of my readers will find many additional meanings that are personal to you.

All of the images are shadow puppets. These are references to Dr. Carl Jung's concept of "The Shadow," which he developed throughout his long career. "The Shadow" is found in the unconscious psyche of every human being. It contains both good and bad elements. The purpose of simply black and white images, and their shadows, is to leave the most psychic space for you to find the meaning of the images to you in the context of Political Psychology.

Cover Image – The Carousel:

Dr. Jung's work is often represented by the mandala, that circular image, which represents the entire world. The idea of a circle is a reference to both Dr. Jung's work, and the fact that we cannot get off the merry-go-round of life, of which politics is a subset; a carousel occupying only one corner of the carnival of life.

The three riders represent The Trinity, which was another of Dr. Jung's themes throughout his career. It can be referred to as "The Father, Son, and Holy Ghost" as Christians do, or it can represent conservative, progressive, and catalytic political positions—the forces of change, which always exist in our political world.

The traditional politician with the wavy Ronald Reagan style hair rides the elephant, which has long been the symbol of the Republican Party and of conservative values.

The woman rider on the donkey represents the fact that the Democratic Party may field a woman as its candidate for President in 2016. The fact that she is lower in the primary image suggests the dominance of patriarchy in our world, but the shadow image, higher than the rest, represents both the fear of the other parties of the emergence of the feminine principle and the unconscious aspirations of many women, who were disappointed when Hillary Clinton bowed out of the 2008 campaign for President.

The politician in the hat on a horse represents a fundamentalist Christian preacher of the late 19th century, on the far right of the image, is a stand in for all splinter groups of the right wing in American politics. They are catalysts for change. To Republicans they represent an element that is seeking to pull the party farther to the right of conservative thought. To Democrats they represent the old passé ideas, which are trying to undermine the progress toward equal rights of minority groups and women attained in the 20th century.

Section 1 – Political Psychology

Here the fat cat rises in the smoke of a cauldron. At the psychological level, this is a reference to alchemy, which was a major element of Dr. Jung's studies throughout the five decades that followed his "Confrontation with the Unconscious," and again to the mandala, which is circular and contains all of our hopes and fears.

The cauldron represents the alchemical vas, or pot, into which ingredients are placed, the combination of which produces psychological gold or political gold, which here emerges as smoke in the form of the wealthy fat cats of society. Here the ingredients are many of the issues troubling American and global politics.

Section 2 – The Big Lie

The soldiers in the Nazi salute conjure the time of the 20th century, when Adolph Hitler's concept of "The Big Lie" held sway in much of Europe. It is symbolic of the ease with which unscrupulous leaders can regiment society. It is also a reference to crowd psychology, about which Dr. Carl Jung and Nobel Prize laureate Elias Canetti warned.

The dominance of "mass men" is a fundamental theme of Dr. Jung's prodigious oeuvre, and it was a phenomenon fully explained by Mr. Canetti in his seminal book, Crowds and Power, which presents us with sobering realities about the tendencies in all human beings.

Section 3 – Personal Morality

The shepherd is an obvious reference to religion, and its uses and abuses in politics. The leader guides his flock for better or for worse, and the flock contains both white sheep and black sheep in the moral sense. Even the shepherd suggests a touch of evil in his shadow.

Dr. Jung once said that the gathering of 100 brilliant minds in a group resulted in the creation of one fat head. He was therefore adamant that each of us learns to differentiate Good from Evil for ourselves, and question the motives of any leader.

Section 4 – The Tea Party

The tea party derived image is an obvious reference to both the American Tea Party, and the illusions of politics in general. Here the MAD HATTER pours the tea into the air, but it misses its mark.

Section 5 – The War on Women

This image of female targets raises the question of why and how women become the targets of patriarchal culture, society and politics. Men dominate politics and power elites. They only make up half of the population, but they do not share power with women, who compose the other half.

Instead, women are systematically targeted and governed by being silenced, oppressed, and forced into passivity. Men target women as a way to divide and conquer, breaking up cultural systems they do not like, in order to gain more dominance over women, building government and society in the patriarchal forms they prefer.

Section 6 – The Social Contract and Income Disparity

The ballet dancer on the raging bull is symbolic of the unfinished business of the Occupy Wall Street movement, with its many issues relating to the way the global economy is run for the benefit of the 1%, who are the primary patrons of fragile arts like ballet.

Section 7 - Culture Pot Full of Holes

Humpty Dumpty refers to culture, the mandala of our world as an egg, and the fact that he is broken points to the fact that the only thing that doesn't change is change itself. Conservative forces are always trying to put Humpty Dumpty back together again—making the culture as it was in an earlier time. Progressive forces recognize that change is inevitable, and always seek to make a new culture from the old, which is better than the one before. This is a never-ending process, but one thing is perfectly clear—no one can put Humpty Dumpty back together again.

Section 8 – Mythologizing

Even symbols made of stone, as the statues of Mr. Rushmore are, become weathered and passé. We mythologize that the men represented were somehow heroic. While yes, they were, they were also mortal men with many flaws.

There is a reason why so many black Americans carry the surname Washington and Jefferson. Teddy Roosevelt confiscated Native American lands for the federal government, and is symbolic of the latter part of the conquering of so-called Native Americans by European Americans. Abe Lincoln was a consummate politician, who horse-traded with the best politicians of his day to reach his goals, sometimes at the cost of many future lives.

Washington and Jefferson avoided the issue they called "The Wolf," leaving it to be resolved with blood four score and seven years later at the Battle of Gettysburg. Like politicians today, they knew how to "kick the can down the road."

And there were many other heroes, both men and women, in whose honor no monument was ever built, but who made contributions every bit as important to the development of global society as it is today.

Section 9 – Sweet Land of Liberty

The Statue of Liberty symbolizes the promise of America, to take the poor and wretched from around the world and forge them into a great nation. She represents the promise to allow the human spirit to develop to its full potential, which was the "gold" the alchemists were actually seeking, as Dr. Jung showed us.

But today conservative forces wish to put an end to the promises of America. The changed image of the Statue of Liberty speaks for itself.

BIBLIOGRAPHY

Apollo 13, Produced by Brian Grazer, Directed by Ron Howard, starring Tom Hanks, Kevin Bacon, Bill Paxton, Gary Sinise, and Ed Harris (1995).

ARIKAN, MELTEM, *"Confronting THE BIG LIE,"* Archetype in Action™ Organization, October 17, 2011.

BOLEN, JEAN SHINODA, *Goddesses in Everywoman: Powerful Archetypes in Women's Lives*, Harper Collins, (1984)

BOLEN, JEAN SHINODA, *Gods in Everyman: Archetypes That Shape Men's Lives*, Harper Paperback's (1993)

CONOVER, SKIP, *Tsunami of Blood*, Words Matter, LLC (2007)

DICKENS, CHARLES, *Tale of Two Cities*, (1859).

ESTES, CLARISSA PINKOLA, *Women Who Run with the Wolves*, Ballantine Books (1993)

HUGO, VICTOR, *Les Misérables*, (1862)

JUNG, CARL G., *Answer to Job*, Princeton University Press (2010)

JUNG, CARL G., *Aion, Researches into the Phenomenology of the Self*, Princeton University Press (1979)

JUNG, CARL G., *Civilization in Transition*, Princeton University Press (1970)

JUNG, CARL G., *Man and His Symbols*, Dell (1968)

JUNG, CARL G. *Memories, Dreams, Reflections*, Vintage (1961, 1989)
JUNG, CARL G., *Psychological Types*, Princeton University Press (1923, 1971)

JUNG, CARL G., *Psychology & Religion*, Yale University Press, (1960)

JUNG, CARL G., *Symbols of Transformation*, Princeton University Press (1911-12/1952), audio *Psychology of the Unconscious*, read by Robert Bethune (1911-12).

JUNG, CARL G., *The Red Book*, W. W. Norton & Company, 1st edition (October 19, 2009) from a private collection developed 1913-1930, Sonu Shamdasani (Ed.)

MYERS, ISABEL BRIGGS, *Manual: A Guide to the Development and Use of the Myers-Briggs Type Indicator*, Consulting Psychologists Press (August 1985)

RAFFA, JEAN BENEDICT, *Healing the Sacred Divide: Making Peace with Ourselves, Each Other, and the World*, Larson Publications (2012)

WOOD, GORDON, *Radicalism of the American Revolution*, Vintage (1993)

ABOUT THE AUTHOR

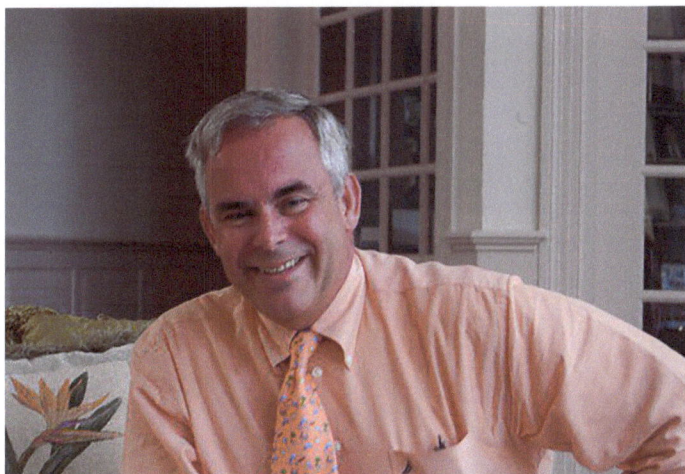

Donald L. (Skip) Conover began his commentary on politics and international affairs in 2005, and supplemented his writing with a detailed study of the work of 20th Century Psychologist Dr. Carl Jung. Today that work continues on the Archetype in Action™ Organization website. Mr. Conover is also the author of *Tsunami of Blood*, which addresses current issues in the Middle East. The 3rd Edition was published for Amazon Kindle Books in September 2014.

Mr. Conover is a graduate of Hamilton College (B.A. 1968). He has been an attorney since 1975, having received a J.D. from the State University of New York in 1974. He also holds an M.B.A. from the William E. Simon Graduate School of Business Administration at The University of Rochester, and was honored as a Distinguished Alumnus in 2005. He was featured in the cover story of Global CEO magazine in June 2008.